Amaeru

Amaeru
The Expression of Reciprocal Dependency Needs in Japanese Politics and Law

Douglas D. Mitchell

The cultural value of reciprocal obligation is so intrinsic in Japanese life that it has only recently come under examination. Yet an understanding of the concept of *amae* is essential to an understanding of Japanese political behavior and law and the decision-making processes in government bureaucracy and corporate structure alike. Here is a complete, careful, and highly readable discussion of *amae,* presenting its essential qualities and tracing it from its origins in early childhood to its pervasive influence in all aspects of Japanese society.

Douglas D. Mitchell received an M.A. in political science from the University of Colorado, where he has taught in the Department of Political Science and the Experimental Studies Program.

Amaeru

Douglas D. Mitchell

Westview Press
Boulder, Colorado

A Westview Replica Edition

Copyright © 1976 by Westview Press, Inc.

Published 1976 in the United States of America by
    Westview Press, Inc.
    1898 Flatiron Court
    Boulder, Colorado 80301
    Frederick A. Praeger, Publisher and Editorial Director

Library of Congress Cataloging in Publication Data
Mitchell, Douglas D.
    Amaeru.

    (Westview replica editions)
    Originally presented as the author's thesis (M.A.), University of Colorado, 1976.
    Bibliography: p. 218
    1. Japan—Politics and government. 2. Politics, Practical. 3. Sociological jurisprudence—History—Japan. 4. Dependency (Psychology).
5. National characteristics, Japanese. I. Title.
JQ1681.M57 1977   301.15'7'0952   76-43354
ISBN 0-89158-710-1

Printed and bound in the United States of America.

TABLE OF CONTENTS

CHAPTER   PAGE

I.   INTRODUCTION.   1

     National Character Studies on Japan . . .   11

          Ruth Benedict.   11
          Maruyama Masao   13
          Nakamura Hajime.   15
          George DeVos   16

II. THE ORIGINS AND PERSONAL DYNAMICS OF
     AMAE.   19

     Child Rearing and Personality Development
     in Japan.   21

          Nursing and Physical Contact   22
          Toilet Training.   26
          Punishment   28
          Sleeping Arrangements.   31
          Summary.   34

     Amae in Adult Attitudes   36

          Amae in Literature   37
          Japanese Cultural Attitude Studies . .   39

     Conclusion.   42

III. RECIPROCAL AMAE AND AUTHORITY RELATIONS .   43

     Mutual Dependency in Mother-Child
          Relationship   44

          Asymmetry of Amae Reciprocity. . . .   45
          Guilt and Achievement Motivation . . .   46
          The Amae Element in On-giri-ninjo. . .   50
          Conclusion   53

     Amae and Authority: Reciprocity of
          Obedience and Indulgence   54

Mother and Father: Authority
  Relations in the Family 55
Rule From Below: Patterns in
  Traditional Japanese Politics . . . 60
Politicization of Emperor's Role . . . 64

The Family-State System 67

Traditional Political Values:
  Linkage Between Ie and Kokutai. . . 68
Emperor Veneration 70

Dependency as the Basis for Authority . . 71

"Lack of Self" 72
"Authoritarianism" 75

Conclusion. 78

IV. AMAE AND GROUP BEHAVIOR IN MAINSTREAM
JAPAN. 80

Introduction. 80

The Bases of Group Formation. 83

The Vertical Structure of Japanese
  Society 83
The Group as a "Frame" 84

Amae and Emotional Unity in the Group . . 86

Life-Time Employment 88
Company Involvement in Family Life . . 91
Style of Leadership. 92
Decision Making without Confrontation. 96

Factionalism. 101

"We" vs. "Them". 103
Functional and Dysfunctional Aspects . 105

Organizational Weaknesses 106
Analyses of Factionalism:
  Summary. 110
Financing Factionalism. 115

The Tenacity of Factions 118

Conclusion: The Explanatory Power of
Amae. 120

V. AMAE AND THE POLITICS OF OPPOSITION . . .   124

The Student in Japanese Society   126

The Role of Amae in Student Activism. . .   129

Permissiveness in a Society of
    Control   129
Student Group Formation.   130
Confrontation and Manipulation   136

From Passive Resistance to
    Active Confrontation   137
The University Crisis of
    1968-1969.   139
Amae and "Victim Consciousness" . .   141

The Boundaries of Violent Opposition .   144
Conclusion   147

Partisan Politics and Problems of
Loyal Opposition.   150

The Liberal Democratic Party and Con-
    trol of the Parliamentary Process .   152
Amae and the Permanent Opposition. . .   158
The 1960 U.S.-Japan Security Treaty
    Crisis.   162

Amae and the Meaning of Japanese
Democracy   168

VI. LAW AND THE VALUES OF AMAE.   173

Amae and Extra-Legal Restraint.   175

Conciliation as a Group Priority
    and Legal Value   178
Contracts in Japan   180

The Amae Relationship   181
Right and Duty.   185

Individualism and Rights Consciousness. .   187

CHAPTER   PAGE

          Selfhood   187
          Individualism.   189

             Citizens' Movements   189
             Rights Litigation and Related
                Gains in Rights Consciousness. . 195

          Response to Activism: Restoring
             the Symmetry of Amae.   198

 VII. CONCLUSION: THE CONCEPT OF AMAE   203

       The Unfolding of Amae: Concrete and
       Conceptual.   206

       Conclusion.   215

BIBLIOGRAPHY.   218

CHAPTER I

INTRODUCTION

In 1971 a Japanese psychoanalyst named Doi Takeo[1]
produced a book which represented the culmination in the
development of his thesis on the fundamental human need
to be dependent. Amae No Kōzō (The Structure of Amae)
was translated into English in 1973 as The Anatomy of
Dependence.[2] The term amae, however, is not easily
understood by non-Japanese. In fact, as will at length
become apparent, there is considerable disagreement even
among Japanese about the precise definition of the word.
Amae is the nominalization of the verb whose citation
form is amaeru (甘える). Although the English transla-
tions for the verb which are given in a popular Japanese-
to-English dictionary bear only some resemblance to the
more technical meanings which Doi has given to it, those
definitions are instructive starting points in gaining
an appreciation for the full range of nuance conveyed
by the word:

---

[1]The names of native Japanese are given here in
the order of customary Japanese usage: surname followed
by given name.

[2]Doi Takeo, The Anatomy of Dependence (Tokyo:
Kodansha Int'l., Ltd., 1973); John Bester, translator.

Amaeru 甘える 1. 〔子供が (applied to a child)〕 behave like a spoilt child. 2. 〔女などが (applied to women)〕 be coquettish. 3. 〔犬などが (applied to dogs, etc.)〕 fawn on 〔a person〕. 4. 〔せびる (synonymous with sebiru, to importune)〕 coax.... 5. 〔好意・親切などが (applied to good will, kindness, etc.)〕 avail oneself of, take advantage of.[1]

In its first four definitions, amaeru shows a direct and obvious relationship to an adjective of the same root,[2] amai (甘い), meaning sweet or sugary. From evidence collected by the author,[3] it appears to be in these meanings that Japanese are most familiar with the term amaeru and most accustomed to using it.[4]

For Doi's purposes, however, and for our purposes here, the fifth definition is most meaningful: to avail oneself of some kindness or favor; to take advantage of a person's good will. It is this simple definition which

_____

[1]Sanseido's New Concise Japanese-English Dictionary (Tokyo: Sanseido Press, 1967), p. 15.

[2]Amai (甘い). See Andrew N. Nelson, Japanese-English Character Dictionary (Tokyo: Tuttle, 1974), p. 615-616. Doi speculates that the root of amai might originally have been identified with the root of the same pronunciation meaning the heavens; p. 73.

[3]A questionnaire to determine the prevalent understandings of Amae was given by the writer to a sample of American students and Japanese instructors at the Japanese Language School, Middlebury College, Vermont, in the summer of 1975. Interestingly, the almost universal response of the Japanese, upon seeing the subject matter of the questionnaire, was to intone, "fukuzatsu" ("complex").

[4]For example, children may often be referred to as amaekko or amattare, "spoiled child"; amato is a sweet tooth.

should be kept in mind as we proceed to explore the full meaning of the term.

In an odd socio-linguistic twist, this last meaning for amaeru is related to yet another definition for amai, but inversely. Amai, in its second meaning is "厳しくない (not strict)/ indulgent, generous."[1] Those two adjectives do not describe the behavior of a person who amaeru's; rather, they are the attributes of a person who will likely be the object of amaeru. Generally, to amaeru[2] is to behave self-indulgently in a special relationship with another person or group of people.[3] The one will amaeru; the other will be amai in response.[4]

This is the first lesson about amae: both roles, the indulgent and the indulger, are necessary for the

---

[1]Sanseido, p. 15.

[2]For simplicity's sake, the citation form of the Japanese verb will be used in the text at points where an English verb would be called for--in any of the forms infinitive, third person singular or third person plural, and gerund.

[3]Doi, p. 24. "...thus if A is said to be amai to B, it means that he allows B to amaeru, i.e., to behave self-indulgently, presuming on some special relationship that exists between the two."

[4]Lebra uses the term amayakasu, "to indulge" (a child). Takie Sugiyama Lebra, "Reciprocity and the Asymmetric Principle: An Analytical Reappraisal of the Japanese Concept of On," in Japanese Culture and Behavior, Takie Sugiyama Lebra and William Lebra, eds., (Honolulu: University Press of Hawaii, 1974), p. 199.

dependency pattern known as amae to be in operation.
The reciprocity of those roles is an important subject
to be considered herein.

Beyond the consensus which exists on the dyadic
nature of the amae relationship, there seems to be considerable disagreement. Scholars from different disciplines have provided new, and always slightly varied
interpretations of amae, its origins, its nature, and
its significance. Many, however, have brought valuable
insights to bear which have enlarged our understanding
of amae and which make it possible for amae to be used
with increasing sophistication as a tool for analysis
of Japan and its people.

Already in discussing amae, I have used the term
in reference to needs, relationships, behavior, and a
pattern--or, in other words, as an analytic construct on
the one hand and as an empirical phenomenon on the
other. The task of this study, in a sense, is to draw
the two together. Until it has finally succeeded, however, a convention is needed for clarity's sake. The
convention which is offered here is as follows: Amae
signifies the need or complex of needs which leads a
person to behave in a certain way. Amaeru is that behavior; it is to act in such a way that those needs are
being filled in a relationship, or that they are being
expressed in such a way that a relationship is being
established in which they will be filled.

Some of the ambiguity surrounding amae today arises from the overly general interpretations which Doi has made of amae. His ideas on the subject have found expression in a variety of publications, of which The Anatomy of Dependence is only the latest to be translated in English. Of first great impact outside the field of psychiatry was his article entitled, "Amae: A Key Concept for Understanding Japanese Personality Structure."[1]

Doi suspects that amae is a universal human need, corresponding, for example, to the western psychiatric notion of "passive object love." The desire to "depend and presume upon another's benevolence" is carried over into adult life from its first realization in the infant's relationship to his mother. The existence of a uniquely Japanese term to express this need, however, suggests a basic psychological difference between Japan and other countries. That psychological difference is explained by Doi in terms of the unique, persisting strength among Japanese of amae. This psychological characteristic, Doi deduces, "indicates that there is a social sanction in Japanese society for expressing the wish to amaeru.... In other words, in Japanese society

---

[1]Doi Takeo, "Amae: A Key Concept for Understanding Japanese Personality Structure," Japanese Culture, eds. Robert J. Smith and Richard K. Beardsley (Chicago: Aldine Publishing Co., 1962); pp. 132-139.

parental dependency is fostered, and this behavior pattern is even institutionalized into its social structure...."[1] Such institutionalization creates channels through which the desire to amaeru may be gratified. The need to be dependent, then, is seen as a positive emotion which finds expression in a multitude of formalized social relationships. At the same time, unrestrained amae is seen as a potentially destructive force in Japanese society.[2] Especially today, given the loss of restraints on amaeru in the post-war years, the challenge to Japanese society is clearly posed: to find new channels through which amae may find creative expression, or suffer the consequences of its destructive influence.

The pathological potential in amae is elaborated on in Doi's book, The Anatomy of Dependence. In it, he expands his thoughts on the relationship between amae and a broad spectrum of neuroses (obsession, compulsion, hypochondria, homosexuality). He also develops further the linguistic analysis of a number of psychological terms which he considers to be derivative of amae in either its expression or frustration. But most notably,

---

[1]Doi (1962), p. 136.

[2]The negative element in Doi's discussion of amae must stem largely from his clinical experience with pathological amaeru among psychiatric patients.

he undertakes an exposition of amae in which he makes much bolder claims than before for the ubiquity of amae in the personal, social, and cultural experience of the Japanese.

> /The Japanese/ primal experience gave rise, on the one hand, to the emperor system and the family-centered society that is related to it, and, on the other, fostered the peculiarly Japanese ways of feeling and thinking. Now I would suggest that the basic emotional urge that has fashioned the Japanese for two thousand years is none other than the amae mentality.[1]

Having introduced the ideas of today's leading expositor of amae, I will go on to substantiate many of his conclusions, to challenge some, and to use others as starting points for my own inquiry into the nature of amae and its political manifestations. The objective will be to show, in a more systematic and detailed way than Doi has, the ways in which amae operates in the Japanese political realm. It will be argued that amae is significant to the study of Japanese politics not simply as another aspect of the political culture, but as a motivational factor which underlies many characteristics already recognized and which explains more successfully than any other concept a great deal of key Japanese political behavior.

Chapter 2 will describe the family relationships and the child-rearing practices which are both the

---

[1]Doi (1973), p. 82.

foundations and, for our purposes here, the first illus-
trations of amae. I will review the various studies
that have been made of personality development in Japan,
particularly in the context of family life and childhood; and their conclusions will be presented in respect
to two issues: 1) The significance of early childhood
experience in developing the emotional needs known as
amae, and 2) The continuing influence of amae on adult
behavior.

Having established amae as a motivational factor
with almost universal impact among Japanese people, I
will devote the next three chapters to exploring the
ways in which amae affects political behavior in particular. First to be considered is attitude toward
authority in general; and salient in Japanese politics
has been the attitude toward the Emperor in particular.
Chapter 3, therefore, will describe the historical role
of the Emperor, and his relationship to the family-state
system, particularly as that system took shape under the
ideologies of Meiji and pre-war Japan. The events surrounding the Japanese surrender in the defeat of 1945,
which changed the role of the Emperor and the popular
perception of him, will be shown to have importance for
the study of the "amae ideology." And political norms
such as filial piety and duty to repay kindness will be
analyzed as important parts of that ideology.

With the _amae_ content in the primordial political
relationship in pre-World War II Japan clearly shown, I
will demonstrate its continuing existence in post-war
Japanese politics. My examples will be drawn from three
general areas of political behavior in Japan. To be considered in Chapter 4 are several significant aspects of
what is often referred to as "mainstream" political and
organizational behavior in Japan. Particularly instructive examples of the operation of _amae_ are to be found in
the decision-making processes in government bureaucracy
and corporate structure alike.

Also Chapter 4 will focus on perhaps the most con-
troversial issue within Japanese political parties, both
mainstream and anti-mainstream: factionalism. Over the
years, much has been written in the way of description of
and partial explanation for the strong factional basis of
parties in Japan, with attention directed usually toward
traditional patterns of "bossism," the mandates of hierarchical group formation, or the real-_politik_ of fund
raising in corporate-dominated election campaigns. I
will argue, however, that as helpful as these and other
factors may be in explaining the dynamics of factionalism, none of them succeed in offering a needed explanation for the tenacity with which the Japanese have clung
to this characteristic mode of political life. Other
paradigms have answered the "How?" of factionalism;
amae alone answers the "Why?" This it achieves by

identifying the shared emotional need which no other
form of political organization within a parliamentary
system could meet so well.

Second to be considered, in Chapter 5, will be
the politics of opposition in Japan, to include the role
and tactics of minority parties, along with their support organizations in labor federations, and the characteristics of student radicalism. Although the two are
distinctively separate actors on the Japanese political
stage, it will be shown that the relationship which each
has--or attempts to maintain--to society as a whole
gives the two a common basis in amae.

All those characteristics of Japanese politics
which will be considered are, inevitably, undergoing the
change that new generations and new ideas must introduce. If existing patterns and institutions are, as I
will argue, vital channels for constructive expression
of amae, what will be the effect of such changes?
Answers to that question raise, in turn, the possibility
that amae may be of decreasing importance as a political
value in Japan. In Chapter 6 that possibility will be
weighed in the context of post-war developments in two
particular areas where evidence has been found that significant value changes are occurring. The first is the
evolution of legal concepts, especially as they relate
to the development of rights consciousness within the

constitutional framework of Japanese democracy. The
second related feature is the growth of voluntary organizations, as evidenced in the new political activism of
citizens' movements.

Although no definite conclusions can be drawn
about the ascendency or descendency of amae today, our
consideration of amae in a changing society raises,
finally, several theoretical questions about personality,
culture, and politics. The concluding chapter, therefore, looks back over the picture of amae as it has
emerged and attempts to clarify in a theoretical and
comparative framework how amae fits, modifies, or
refutes prevalent modes of thinking among the social
sciences in such areas as socialization, psycho-cultural
studies, and functionalism.

All told, the value which amae holds out to students of Japanese politics is its superior explanatory
power, and to all the social sciences, a clear example
of linkage among them.

A. National Character Studies on Japan

1. Ruth Benedict

With an impact second only to Commodore Perry's
on the level of information about Japan, Ruth Benedict
in 1946 opened the door on Japan for those Americans
who cared to step through. As a cultural anthropologist
drawing on the psychoanalytic interpretations in whose

application she was a pioneer, she produced the first
among many attempts to present a psycho-cultural por-
trait of the Japanese people as a whole.[1]

To that point, Japan had been known to Americans
mainly as an enemy. Her effort to explain the apparent
fanaticism of a people in terms of a rigid authoritarianism operating in a culture pervaded by consciousness of
shame (haji) stirred considerable controversy. In her
study, Benedict identified shame as the most significant
dynamic in Japanese social relations; the fear of bringing shame upon oneself or one's family was seen as the
key emotion in Japanese culture. And the family's effec-
tiveness in developing that fear in its children assured
their responsiveness as adults within the authoritarian
and hierarchical social structure of Japan.[2]

Benedict appreciated the great significance in
Japan of loyalty and duty and recognized the strong network of obligations and personal indebtedness which was
a determinative factor in the lives of all Japanese. As
a practical explanation for the existence of such
strongly enforced conventions of social interaction,

---

[1]Ruth Benedict, The Chrysanthemum and the Sword
(Boston: Houghton-Mifflin, 1946).

[2]Remarkably, Benedict's study was accomplished
without the benefit of field research. In it, she distinguishes between the cultures of "shame" and "guilt"
(pp. 222-223). Doi (1973) takes exception to her characterization of Japan as a "shame" culture (pp. 48-50).

Benedict pointed to the isolating topographies of the
Japanese islands and the communal economies of traditional agrarian villages. Only in a limited way does she
appear to have recognized those codes of behavior as
restraints on emotions; and the critical emotion was
shame.

2. Maruyama Masao

In the aftermath of defeat, some Japanese scholars
seemed compelled to retrace the path of their own
national self-destruction. Characteristically, their
introspective attempts to discover the seeds of disaster
and to explain their taking root in Japanese soil were
formulated in the rigid analytical categories dictated
by the Marxist determinism which was then flourishing in
Japanese academics. A leading example is Maruyama Masao,
who saw the political pressures leading to war in terms
of inevitable structural conflicts created by the process
of modernization.[1]

A second theme running through Maruyama's writing
is to explore the possibilities for mature democracy in
post-war Japan.[2] In a departure from his predominantly

---

[1]Maruyama Masao, Thought and Behavior in Modern
Japanese Politics (London: Oxford University Press,
1963); Ivan Morris, ed.

[2]This theme, inseparable from the more muted and
sensitive question of whether or not a more democratic
response might have been possible to those pre-war pressures, is the logical concomitant to the first. It reflects the intellectuals' self-conscious awareness of
their pre-war role and of the need to reestablish their
untarnished image. See Tim J. Schmitz, "Japanese Intellectuals: Reactions in Modernization," Unpublished, University of Colorado, 1972.

materialistic approach, he addresses with obvious feeling the problems which appear to be presented by the
Japanese national character. Maruyama shows considerable concern--and criticism--for what he calls "pre-
modern" characteristics of Japanese society, as in the
following selection:

> Here the type of man exalted is one whose life is
> cluttered up with all sorts of "relationships."
> He is not thought of as an independent entity,
> but as part and parcel of his own concrete envi-
> ronment. For him, morality and standards of
> behavior hold good only in "established" relation-
> ships with people. In these relationships he has
> a strong sense of honor, but at the same time he
> behaves disgracefully toward strangers or toward
> people with whom he has no "defined" association.
> The strength of his control over, or influence
> on, another person depends on his position,
> status, family standing, or "face."[1]

That description introduces several acknowledged characteristics of Japanese interpersonal relations, which
will be treated more fully below. But his identification
of status and "face" as important characteristics seems
to uphold Benedict's conclusions about the operation of
shame in the Japanese social hierarchy. In addition,
he alludes strongly to the psycho-cultural theme bril-
liantly developed by another Japanese scholar, Nakamura
Hajime.[2]

---

[1]Maruyama, pp. 257-258.

[2]Nakamura Hajime, Ways of Thinking of Eastern
Peoples (Honolulu: University Press of Hawaii, 1964);
Philip Wiener, ed.

3. Nakamura Hajime

Nakamura also seems to be at pains to explain the disgrace brought on his country by defeat. His comprehensive study of the "ways of thinking" of four Asian nations is primarily a study of religious cultures; and its encyclopeadic nature does not suggest at first any intent for it to be an apology for the particular religious statism which presided over the rise and fall of imperial Japan. Nevertheless, in his discussion of Japan, he seems to tie the book together very inconspicuously along just that line:

> ...just as religion was the basis of the ethical thinking of the Indians, and family the basis of the practical morals of the Chinese, so the state was the basis of all thought in the Japanese....[1]

Nakamura reaches this conclusion by his development of one predominant characteristic of the Japanese people, their preference for operating within what he calls the "limited social nexus," or, expressed in another way, "the general tendency in Japanese thinking, especially in the past, to overlook the universal and to lay stress upon an exclusive human nexus."[2]

Nakamura finds several features of interpersonal relations and group loyalty to be the consequences or manifestations of this key characteristic; those features will be discussed in ensuing chapters. It

---

[1]Ibid., p. 448.   [2]Ibid.

suffices at this point to take note of two facts: first, Nakamura has tried to portray a "way of thinking" as a characteristic of Japanese people; and second, he has concluded that such a characteristic "has a close relation to" Japanese political behavior.[1]

4. George DeVos

If military defeat in World War II was an unparalleled event in the history of Japan, so also was its 180-degree turnabout away from ruin and toward unrivaled reconstruction. The Japanese "phenomenon" of post-war industrialization and economic growth seems to have provided the impetus for a second generation of national character studies, represented by the work of George DeVos and others.[2] These studies have characteristically focused on the "achievement orientation" or related attitudes shared among the Japanese which might suggest a unique motivational factor responsible for the accomplishments of the Japanese nation. Similar interpretations have been made of the psycho-cultural foundations for rapid change in Meiji Japan. Inherent in this line of inquiry is the assumption of a cultural continuity in value orientations over the period of both national experiences.

---

[1]Ibid.

[2]George A. DeVos, Socialization for Achievement (Berkeley: University of California Press, 1973).

In identifying "achievement motivation" as the
outstanding characteristic of the Japanese cultural psychology, DeVos follows Ruth Benedict and others in his
attention to the psychodynamics of the "indebtedness"
expressed in the term "on".[1] For DeVos, however, the
significance of on is that it points not to concern with
shame or "face", but to internalized guilt as the key
motivational factor.[2]

> I would regard instrumental concerns with inade-
> quacy and expressive concerns with appreciation
> less prepotent when they are viewed within a
> total context of interpersonal concerns, including
> instrumental concerns with achievement and
> responsibility, and expressive concerns with
> interdependency and nurturance. If so perceived,
> Japan can hardly be called a "shame" culture. In
> fact, problems related to "guilt" are culturally
> much more in evidence.[3]

DeVos's work has brought innovation to the study
of Japanese psychoculture; and we will be returning
shortly to a more detailed explanation of his interpretations, especially in relation to the "interdependency
and nurturance" noted above. But DeVos's conclusion,
like others, invites further inquiry into the Japanese
personality in relation to "normative role behavior:"

> In the psychological motivation underlying
> on,... one finds the key to the Japanese need to

---

[1]This term is discussed fully below, pages 50-52.

[2]DeVos, p. 9.   [3]Ibid., p. 30-31.

> adhere to life-long patterns of dedication to socially prescribed roles and their attendant goals.[1]

Here, finally, we find an attempt to identify the emotional underpinnings of the national characteristics noted by others. Doi has argued that _amae_ is that motivation. Sufficient study has been made of personality development in Japan to allow that argument to be defended. The following chapter will summarize the existing body of research and will show how _amae_ is developed in childhood, and how it is expressed in adult behavior in family life.

---

[1] _Ibid._, p. 9.

CHAPTER II

THE ORIGINS AND PERSONAL DYNAMICS OF <u>AMAE</u>

The process of child rearing in Japan is markedly different from that generally observed in the United States. The difference in approach is symbolized--even before the process begins--by the customary practice among Japanese hospitals of presenting the mother with a box containing the umbilical cord of her new child. Japanese upbringing emphasizes symbiosis, almost as though the cord were still attached. In American childhood, individuation is emphasized. Dependency versus independence; passivity versus self-assertiveness; group-identity versus self-identity: these are the themes of contrast between the characteristics of Japanese and American maturation processes, as well as their respective communication styles and patterns of political behavior in general. Leaving comparison for the moment, let us examine in some detail the usual Japanese patterns of child-rearing and family life, which direct the child toward attitudes and behavior characterized by dependency, passivity, and identification with a social unit larger than himself. These characteristics express rather well the essence of <u>amae</u> in the Japanese personality.

Richard Beardsley attempts to clarify the connotations of _amaeru_ by distinguishing three different ways to _amaeru_. Each type of behavior solicits a somewhat different response; but all express the dependency orientation which has its origins in childhood.[1] 1) "To be cuddlesome, coquettish, lovable" is behavior which invites love; DeVos defines this as "the passive-manipulative ability to induce in others an active desire to love and care for one."[2] It is in this sense that _amaeru_ is most commonly applied to endearing behavior by Japanese women. 2) "To take advantage (of someone)" is behavior which feeds on another person; it is in this sense that having a dependent relationship with a person (or a group of people) creates, in a very real sense, a realm of greater freedom than one might otherwise enjoy in Japanese society. And finally, 3) "to act like a spoiled child" is often the form of behavior which "taking advantage of someone" assumes. The objective of this sort of _amaeru_, according to Beardsley, is to "selfishly demand attention." As will be seen in later chapters, this behavior is by no means limited to spoiled children.

---

[1] Richard K. Beardsley, "Personality Psychology," Twelve Doors to Japan, John W. Hall and Richard K. Beardsley, eds., (New York: McGraw-Hill, 1965), pp. 350-383.

[2] DeVos, p. 549.

The first point to be made about childhood in the typical Japanese family is that the children are indeed indulged.[1] So attentively are the desires of children catered to during their early years that there is little need for a small child to amaeru in this last, active sense. Rather, it is in later childhood and adulthood that people may be said to impose childishly or selfishly.[2] Even so, this behavior springs psychologically from the very fact that, as small children, Japanese are led to expect nurturance, attention, and love; they are spoiled; they are, in other words encouraged to amaeru.

A. Child Rearing and Personality Development in Japan

This encouragement toward the emotional dependency of amae has been studied fairly widely in several contexts. The following discussion includes studies of nursing and physical contact, toilet training, punishment, and sleeping arrangements in Japan.

---

[1]For the Japanese, childhood and old age are the periods of greatest indulgence; both times are regarded with pleasure as those when needs are most catered to.

[2]In fact, it might be just as well to discard the term "amaeru" in describing the behavior of infants and to agree with Harumi Befu /Japan: An Anthropological Introduction (San Francisco: Chandler Publishing Co., 1971)/ that "the indulgence in parental love is the genesis of amae" (p. 159; emphasis mine), and not actually an expression of it. Doi (1973, p. 7), however, argues that infantile behavior is the prototype of amaeru.

1. Nursing and Physical Contact

The Japanese mother characteristically devotes herself to preventing, or at least relieving any anxiety which might develop in the infant. This she achieves by immediate gratification of the child's desire to nurse, and by maximum possible physical contact between mother and child at other times. The primary communication between the two is not verbal, but physical; and the mother will often secure the baby to her back as she goes about her routine, both inside and outside the house.

William Caudill has done a considerable amount of field work in the United States and Japan with results that substantiate Doi's claim for amae as the key source of differences between the pathologies of an American and a Japanese personality. The purpose of much of Caudill's research has been to identify those cultural characteristics which might produce psychodynamic conflicts of a sort that would require different psychiatric treatment from those encountered in American patients.[1] That line of inquiry led him and Helen Weinstein to conduct a comparative study of child-rearing

[1]See, for example, William Caudill and Harry A. Scarr, "Japanese Value Orientation and Cultural Change," Ethnology, 1 (1962), 53-91.

practices in Japan and the United States.[1] From their
recording of the interaction of thirty mother-and-
child pairs in each country, in categories measuring
both infant behavior and caretaker behavior, they found
no significant differences in respect to the amount of
time spent feeding, sleeping, or vocalizing. A significant difference, however, was found in those vari-
ables which showed the American baby to be more active,
exploratory, and "happily vocal" than his Japanese counterpart. Japanese mothers all spent more time with
their infants than did the Americans, and they employed
physical contact in preference to verbal interaction
with the child. In contrast to the American mother,
who cultivated a more active and assertive child, the
Japanese mother encouraged the development of a passive,
contented child. Without rendering judgment as to any
causal relationship involved, Caudill and Weinstein
point out, "these patterns of behavior, so early learned
by the infant, are in line with with differing expectations for later behavior in the two cultures as the
child grows to be an adult."[2]

---

[1]William Caudill and Helen Weinstein, "Maternal
Care and Infant Behavior in Japan and America,"
Psychiatry, 32 (1969), 12-43.

[2]Ibid., p. 264.

An early study by Betty Lanham[1] presented a wider
variety of information collected by the use of a questionnaire distributed among parents in the city of
Kainan. In general, Lanham found:

> Toilet training may not be too different from
> what occurs in the United States. Weaning is
> much more protracted or deferred. As reported
> there is perhaps more similarity than dissimi-
> larity with respect to punishment.[2]

In comparing the two cultures, she reiterates the theme
which was characteristic of most studies from the period
of the early 1950's: "The American child is less often
shamed and practically never with respect to disgrace
of his family."

In the area of nursing habits, Japanese children
were found to nurse much later into childhood than their
American counterparts, with weaning being completed in
no cases (out of 355) within the first year after birth,
and in two cases, as late as the sixth year. The modal
age for completion of weaning was found to lie between
one year-nine months and two years-two months. Although
data showed weaning to be completed normally within six

1Betty B. Lanham, "Aspects of Child Care in Japan:
A Preliminary Report," Personal Character and Cultural
Milieu, Douglas G. Haring, ed., (Syracuse: Syracuse
University Press, 1956), pp. 565-583.

2Ibid., p. 581.

months after initiation, Lanham points out that "weaned" children do return to the breast occasionally.[1] This habit fits within the Japanese pattern of breast-feeding "on demand" rather than "on schedule." These practices reflect an approach to nursing at the time and place of the study which prolongs a period of oral gratification and dependency in a passive love relationship for the Japanese child.

If, as John Bester, Doi's translator, states, "amae refers initially to the feeling that all normal infants at the breast harbor toward the mother--dependence, the desire to be passively loved, the unwillingness to be separated from the warm mother-child circle...."[2] then this extended period of nursing

---

[1]Ibid., p. 567. Selection of the sample studied by Lanham would appear to have excluded mothers who might have been forced to abandon breast feeding for reasons other than choice. An example is phlebitis, an inflammation of higher incidence among Japanese than American mothers, which prevents nursing.

[2]Doi (1973); Introduction by John Bester, p. 7.

clearly has the effect of reinforcing those feelings,
and of encouraging the development of amae.[1]

2. Toilet Training

Toilet training has been dealt with in western
psychoanalytic literature on childhood development as
the second major episode in the psychosexual development
of the personality. Western psychiatry has generally
held that it is within the context of toilet training
that the child first experiences the nurturing parent as
an authority figure, and first discovers that his per-
ceptual world (i.e., parents) exists not to satisfy him
alone, but to have its own demands met as well. In
Japan, this stage in child-rearing, like weaning, is
handled in such a way that no demands are placed on the
child, the child's discomfort is avoided, and nothing
transpires to disrupt the world in which the child finds
himself totally cared for by his mother. In fact,

---

[1]The role of nursing in the development of amae
raises questions about its "oral" character. Although
the psychoanalytic background of Doi might well lead one
to suspect a Freudian interpretation of oral fixation to
be offered as the clinical explanation for psychopatholo-
gies surrounding amae, the effect of amae on adult behavior is in fact the opposite from that classical formulation. Whereas the western "oral" personality seeks
through neurotic behavior to compensate for the lack of
gratification of his childhood oral needs, the Japanese
amae personality attempts to perpetuate that relationship of dependency in which the expression of his oral
needs were not only met with gratification, but were
encouraged.

Vogel goes so far as to characterize toilet-training in Japan as "mother training."[1]

The practice consists primarily of the mother's identifying a schedule or recognizing signals so that she can catch the child before he urinates or defecates, and hold him over a potty or a gutter at the right time. Many mothers will even watch the child at night as well as during the day.

> Often by the age of one and certainly by the age of two, by some combination of child-signaling and mother-training, the child is dry.... Toilet training is not viewed as a struggle by which the mother imposes her will. Rather, the mother simply is helping the child to prevent the discomfort that comes from being wet or soiled.[2]

According to Lanham, toilet training is often delayed until the child reaches the age to be able to go by himself.[3] Lanham's questionnaire responses seemed to indicate a significant instance of punishment by parents when a child soiled himself, although she does make clear, "Punishment may be intended to indicate disapproval and not designed to hurt.[4] Vogel's conclusions to the contrary, however, are supported by

---

[1]Ezra F. Vogel, Japan's New Middle Class (Berkeley: University of California Press, 1963), p. 247.

[2]Ibid., p. 248.   [3]Lanham, p. 568.

[4]Ibid., p. 567.

Edward and Margaret Norbeck's study of child-rearing in a different Japanese community:[1]

> The infant is not shaken, scolded, or subjected
> to any other kind of harsh treatment as a signal
> or as a punishment when diapers are soiled....
> After a child has begun to speak, verbal admoni-
> tion to inform the mother before the event
> occurs is repeated every time the child soils
> itself.[2]

3. Punishment

Disciplinary measures are, of course, taken in any family. But in Japan, physical punishment is but one, and not a favored means of correcting a child's inappropriate behavior. Harumi Befu identifies three traditionally prevalent means of scolding a misbehaving child: the threat of supernatural sanction, the threat of personal shame, and the threat of police arrest.[3] When resorted to, punishments include isolation, ridicule, and spanking.

The critical consideration in mother-child disciplinary interaction appears to be to avoid any action which might be interpreted as a withdrawal of maternal

---

[1]Edward and Margaret Norbeck, "Child Training in a Japanese Fishing Community," Personal Character and Cultural Milieu, Douglas G. Haring, ed., (Syracuse: Syracuse University Press, 1956), pp. 651-673.

[2]Ibid., pp. 657-658.

[3]Befu, p. 158. The last, especially, is admittedly obsolete. A traditional practice now virtually abandoned is a process of superficial cauterization called a "moxa" treatment.

affection. For that reason, according to Befu, neither physical punishment nor physical separation from the mother is resorted to as a means of social control.[1] Characteristically, more indulgent forms of control are used to gain compliance and desired behavior from a child. Out of fifty responses to Lanham's question on how parents obtained compliance from their children, twenty-nine answered that they explained to the child why he should refrain from the activity concerned.[2] Lanham also catalogues the pantheon of ghosts and deities whose intervention might be threatened for recurring disobedience;[3] but the Norbecks indicate that this form of threat is declining in use.[4] Finally, giving sweets (literally, _amai_) as an inducement to compliance is a method which all researchers have documented.[5] Befu notes that giving sweets is regarded as a means of last resort, preceded even by the parents' pleading and begging with the child to behave correctly.[6]

------

[1]_Ibid._, p. 153. This is not to say that outright disobedience goes unpunished. In teaching proper behavior, however, parents are likely to avoid creating the situation in which the child's response must be either "obedient" or "disobedient."

[2]Lanham, p. 574.   [3]_Ibid._, pp. 575-577.

[4]Norbeck, p. 660.

[5]Lanham, p. 578; Norbeck, pp. 661-662.

[6]Befu, p. 157.

At this point, it is important to make explicit
what "correct behavior" entails for the Japanese child:
conformity, and perhaps passivity. Lanham shows that
foremost among the first disciplines in which a young
child is instructed are the courtesies of bowing,
expressing gratitude, greeting strangers, and being
quiet. Principal sanctions are against quarreling with
others or talking back to parents.[1] The Norbecks speak
of "non-conformance" as the sole reason for disciplinary
action.[2]

Japanese parents do not seek to develop an independent or self-assertive child; they are concerned
overwhelmingly with developing in the child an appreciation for the need to behave in conformance with the
standards that are observed by everyone old enough to
know them. It is out of this concern that shame is put
to use as another means of social control of children.

The use of shame as an incentive to proper behavior is generally characteristic of a period in childhood which follows the period of greatest indulgence.

> Until a child enters primary school at the age
> of six, it is treated with great indulgence.
> Behavior is sanctioned by punishment and reward
> as soon as it has learned to comprehend words or
> action; greater conformance to patterns consid-
> ered proper is demanded of girls than of boys.
> Tolerance toward children of both sexes, however,
> is the rule. A small child "has no sense" and

---

[1]Lanham, pp. 572-574.   [2]Norbeck, p. 660.

conformance to the standards imposed upon older
children and adults cannot be expected.[1]

When the time comes, however, the importance of conformance is unambiguously communicated to older children by
the central message inherent in the typical rebuke,
"People will laugh at you." This message has the additional advantage of locating the source of ridicule--
and ultimately, rejection--outside the family, and maintaining the family as a nurturant one.[2] Also, at a later
stage, as will be discussed, the message is easily modi-
fied to become, "People will laugh at us." It is in the
distinction between the two phrasings--"you" as opposed
to "us"--that the crux of the difference between "shame"
and "guilt" in Japanese motivation may be found. Amae
is significant to that distinction.[3]

4. Sleeping Arrangements

A final, and most distinctive characteristic of
Japanese child-rearing practice is the sleeping arrangements customarily followed in the Japanese family. Within days after an infant has been brought home, it will

---

[1]Norbeck, p. 660.

[2]Befu points out that, for the same reason,
mothers may ask a teacher to admonish a particularly
recalcitrant child. "The effect of this recourse is that
the mother succeeds in avoiding discharge of a great
amount of negative affect upon the child" (p. 158).

[3]The distinction between shame and guilt in the
light of amae is discussed below, pp. 52-53.

be sleeping in the bedding with the mother and father. Many children will continue to sleep with an adult relative, if not with the parents themselves, until puberty and even beyond.

The most intensive study of sleeping arrangements in the Japanese family has been conducted by William Caudill and David Plath, who present a detailed account of the many variations in sleeping configurations encountered among 323 households considered.[1] In distinguishing seven general stages of sleeping patterns in the "life cycle" of a nuclear family, they reached several conclusions which are significant to the parent-child relationship, and to amae. When sleeping space permitted, a young child would sleep in a room separate from the parents. For children between the ages of one and five, such cases represented only two percent of that age group. Ninety-one percent slept with either parents or an older relation; the remaining seven percent slept with brothers or sisters.[2]

Those figures reflect the pattern of sleeping arrangements which the researchers discovered: that with the arrival of a second child, who would normally

---

[1]William Caudill and David Plath, "Who Sleeps by Whom? Parent-Child Involvement in Urban Japanese Families," Psychiatry, 29 (1966), 344-366.

[2]Ibid., 351.

be expected to sleep with the mother, the first child is not deprived of an adult sleeping partner. In some cases, all four may sleep in the same room; room size, however, tends to make this alternative undesirable. Understandably, parent couples prefer not to separate; and when an aunt or grandmother is living in the house, the older child will be sent to sleep with her. Where a kinswoman is not available, parents will sleep in separate rooms, each with a child.[1]

In two cases considered, an older child slept alone even though a mother surrogate was available. But in the overwhelming majority of cases, the pattern is clear, and it continues with the addition of a third or even fourth child: that is, until the age of fifteen, a Japanese child has a fifty percent chance of sleeping with one or both parents.[2]

---

[1]Ibid., 353-354.

[2]Ibid., 358-359.
    By taking into consideration the variations in physical arrangements and bedding styles used in Japan, Caudill and Plath were also able to conclude that even after an older child has made the transition required by the arrival of an infant, he remains in a position of greater "access" to the parents than the infant's. Accordingly, the frustration of amae is avoided.
    Statistics for "access" were computed on a scale using the five following positions: 1) Alone; 2) Other person's room; 3) Parents' room in own bed; 4) Parents' room in own futon; 5) In parents' bedding. The value given each position corresponds to its number.
    The futon is a quilt spread out atop straw mat flooring (tatami), usually laid with edges touching adjacent futon.

Japanese sleeping arrangements clearly reflect a widespread concern that not only the infant but older children as well should remain in a position to be cared for and should not be subjected to isolation, or if feasible, to separation from the parents.

> We conclude that, at the very least, there is little change in access to a parent in sleeping arrangements during the transition from infancy to childhood. In contrast, there is sharp physical separation from the parents during this transition in the urban American family, if indeed such a separation had not already been made in infancy. The relative conception of the path to be followed in the socialization of the young child would seem to be different in the two cultures. In Japan, the path seems to lead toward increasing interdependence with other persons, whereas in America, the path seems to lead toward increasing independence from others.[1]

Caudill and Plath's conclusion supports their argument that "the frequency with which children co-sleep with parents expresses a strong cultural emphasis upon the nurturant aspects of family life...."[2]

5. Summary

Harumi Befu in particular has very concisely described the impact of sleeping arrangements in Japan, and of the other areas of child-rearing which have been presented here. A summary of his explanation for the "emotional patterning" in the Japanese family will serve at this point to restate the conclusions that others have drawn from their research. At the same time, it

_____

[1]Ibid., 360-361. [2]Ibid., 344.

presents what I have found to be one of the most complete
and logically coherent statements of the role of amae in
the development of the Japanese personality.

The parental indulgence of "demand-feeding",
co-sleeping, constant maternal care and frequent physical
contact develop in the child a strong dependence upon
parents for emotional security. Accompanying this
dependency is a fear of isolation.[1] The high level of
tolerance for demanding behavior, the passivity of
toilet-training, the infrequent resort to physical
punishment, and the use, instead, of rational explanation, pleading, or attractive inducements to conform to
standards of behavior--often characterized as externally
imposed--all combine to maintain the parent-child relationship (especially between mother and child) as one in
which anxiety is not produced. The nurturance of family
life in Japan is in direct contrast to the practices in
American families in which independence and its attendant
feelings of insecurity and anxiety are created precisely
within that parent-child relationship. Indulgence,
nurturance, and dependency are the characteristics of
the Japanese parent-child relationship, and to quote
again, "it is this indulgence in parental love that is
the genesis of the behavior labeled amae."[2]

---

[1]Befu, pp. 154-157.   [2]Ibid., p. 159.

Amae, for Befu, represents a conventionalized
way of handling emotions and feelings toward other
people which develops not just from several feeding or
sleeping practices, but from constant and systematic
reinforcement by parents of clearly recognizable modes
of behavior.[1]

B. Amae in Adult Attitudes

In the above discussion of childhood attitudes,
conclusions have been stated that the same feelings and
behavior are "prolonged into and diffused throughout
adult life."[2] Befu states succinctly:[3]

> ...even in adulthood Japanese seek affective
> satisfaction through emotional dependence on
> other individuals with whom the ego is in intimate
> relationship, although such behavior is not
> always identified as being amae.

Caudill and Weinstein, it should be recalled, concluded
in their study that "these patterns of behavior, so
early learned by the infant, are in line with the differing expectations for later behavior in the two cultures as the child grows to be an adult."[4] In order to
support these conclusions, we will take brief note of
amae as it is found in literature and of recent attitude

[1]Ibid., pp. 151-152.

[2]Doi (1973), p. 7 (Introduction by John Bester).

[3]Ibid., p. 160.   [4]Supra., p. 23.

studies conducted among Japanese adults.

1. *Amae* in Literature

Some insights into the daily experience of *amae* among Japanese adults are to be gained from novels. Doi has completed an analysis in Japanese of Natsume Soseki's use of *amae*-related concepts as central themes of interpersonal relations in his novels.[1] Some examples which I have encountered in one novel, *Light and Darkness*,[2] illustrate well how *amaeru* is experienced by a mature Japanese in a personal relationship. Speaking of Tsuda, the protagonist, the narrator explains:

> In a certain sense, he liked being treated as a child by her. For, by being treated in that way, he was able to enjoy a special kind of intimacy with her. And when he examined this intimacy carefully, he discovered that it was, after all, a particular kind that could arise only between a man and a woman. Figuratively speaking, it was similar to the pleasant feeling a man receives when he is suddenly tapped on the back coquettishly by a woman at a tea-house.[3]

This conception of *amae* in its customary usage is reflected in the discontented words of his wife, who sees the interpersonal dependence from her vantage point in the traditionally feminine role in the *amae* relationship.

---

[1] Not available in English.

[2] Soseki Natsume, *Light and Darkness* (Exeter: Peter Owen, Ltd., 1971), V. H. Viglielmo, trans.

[3] *Ibid.*, p. 19.

Thinking aloud in the presence of her aunt, O-Nobu says, "I wonder whether a husband is merely a kind of sponge existing only to soak up affection from his wife."[1]

According to Doi, the only instance in which Soseki actually uses the term amae is in the context of an exchange between Tsuda and his wife over the issue of whether or not to accept an invitation to the theater.[2] In this case as well, the word is found in its limited, characteristically female use by O-Nobu: "Don't worry. I don't particularly care about going to the theater, I just wanted to endear myself to you" (amaeru).[3]

Another exchange takes place at a hospital where Tsuda is convalescing from an operation. O-Nobu is clearly feeling uncomfortable about fulfilling the burdensome role of tsukisoi--itself an institutionalized role which embodies the nurturant aspects of amae.[4]

Befu's description of the tsukisoi makes clear the primary emotional content in that role. The

---

[1]Ibid., p. 80.   [2]Doi (1973), pp. 81-82.

[3]Soseki, p. 6. Viglielmo's translation of this sentence differs tellingly from Doi's: "I was behaving like a child."

[4]See William Caudill, "Around the Clock Patient Care in Japanese Psychiatric Hospitals: The Role of the Tsukisoi," American Sociological Review, 26 (1961), 204-214.

tsukisoi is an around-the-clock attendant to a hospital patient; her function is to play "a nurturing or expressive role for the patient in satisfying his emotional needs to depend on another person--his need to amaeru, if you will."[1]

From these examples it is clear that amae has been recognized by writers--specifically, Soseki--as a significant motivation for adult behavior. Research in the form of adult attitude and personality studies has provided confirmation of the importance in adult behavior of positive orientations toward amae.

2. Japanese Cultural Attitude Studies

In a bi-lingual study conducted at International Christian University in Tokyo by Dean Barnlund, an attempt was made to distill a "generalized personality" for both Japanese and Americans. Respondents were asked to designate the most characteristic of thirty alternative adjectives from a "role description checklist."[2] The first-order adjectives chosen by Japanese to describe the Japanese personality were "reserved, silent, evasive, formal, cautious, and serious." The adjectives "distant and dependent" were chosen with the

---

[1]Befu, p. 164.

[2]Dean C. Barnlund, Public and Private Self in Japan and the United States (Tokyo: The Simul Press, 1975), p. 49.

next highest frequency. An English translatation of amaeru, "to seek a protective relationship," was included on the checklist. The frequency with which that alternative was chosen leads the author to conclude, "Since 'to seek a protective relationship' resembles or overlaps 'dependent,' it might also be counted among their cultural attributes."[1]

Psycho-cultural differences have been the objects of study in a significant amount of research conducted among Americans of Japanese ancestry.[2] The results of such studies show conclusively that the differences in childhood personality of the sort that has been detailed here are continuous into adult personality.

Walter Fenz and Abe Arkoff, for example, found among Hawaiian college students of caucasian ancestry high orientations toward "dominance, autonomy, aggression, exhibition, and achievement." Test subjects of Japanese ancestry, by contrast, 'were comparatively high on deference and lowest of any group on dominance,

---

[1]Ibid., p. 50.

[2]See, in addition to those discussed, William Caudill and George DeVos, "Achievement, Culture, and Personality: The Case of the Japanese-Americans," American Anthropologist, 58, No. 6 (1956), 1102-1126. Also, Harry Kitano, Japanese Americans: The Evolution of a Subculture (Englewood Cliffs, N.J.: Prentice-Hall, Inc., 1969).

highest in the need for abasement, and low in the need
for aggression. They were also highest in their expression of the need for nurturance.[1]

In her clinical study of first-generation born
Americans of Japanese ancestry (nisei), Charlotte
Babcock gives a psychoanalytic explanation for the conflict which her patients experience from being
encultured, in effect, to two attitudes toward dependency/
passivity.[2] She suggests, "In Japan there may be more
culturally acceptable adult behavioral derivatives of
the passive wishes than appear to be readily available
in the United States."[3] That insight expresses rather
well, in a comparative context, the thrust of Doi's own
findings, namely, that "in Japanese society parental
dependency is fostered and its behavior pattern is even
institutionalized into its social structure, whereas
the opposite tendency prevails in Western society...."[4]

---

[1]Walter Fenz and Abe Arkoff, "Comparative Need
Patterns of Five Ancestry Groups in Hawaii," Journal of
Social Psychology, 58, (1962), 84. Emphasis mine. Note
that what had been measured--and indeed, what is sig-
nificant--is not the need for nurturance, but the
expression of that need.

[2]Charlotte G. Babcock, "Reflections on Dependency
Phenomena as Seen in Nisei in the United States."
Japanese Culture. Robert J. Smith and Richard K.
Beardsley, eds. Chicago: Aldine Publishing Co., 1962;
pp. 172-183.

[3]Ibid., p. 181.   [4]Doi (1962), p. 138.

C. Conclusion

This chapter has confirmed that "there is a continuity and compatability between the child's dependence on his immediate family and the dependence which he later feels toward his school and work groups."[1] A comparison of the child's family environment and the adult's social environment has yet to be made. That comparison begins in Chapter Three, with a discussion of authority relations in the family-state system.

---

[1]Vogel, p. 235. That conclusion has been confirmed, at this point, without specific reference to the various theories about the mechanisms involved.

CHAPTER III

RECIPROCAL AMAE AND AUTHORITY RELATIONS[1]

Although the origins and characteristics of amae
were discussed in Chapter 2, one key characteristic was
intentionally omitted until this point, namely, its
reciprocity. Even in the earliest mother-child relationship, dependency is mutually experienced. In older
childhood as well certain aspects of amae continue to
be mutually expressed in family relations. The child's
identity with the family unit is the first step toward
identification with larger social units within which
amae may operate--ultimately to include the Japanese
"family-state." Correspondingly, emotional needs and
attitudes toward authority that are developed in family

_____

[1]One problem in communicating the experience of
one people in the language of another is the semantical
difficulty arising from value loadings which different
cultures have imparted over time to certain words.
"Authority" seems to be one such word for Americans
(perhaps owing in part to our imprecision in using the
word increasingly to represent what is better called
"power"). Its emotional content conveys coercion and
creates a suspiciousness in the mind of the hearer.
"Authority" is, of course, benign in many other cultures, including English-speaking ones. It is in its
meaning of "right to rule" that it is used here. This
chapter shows how the Japanese sense of this "right to
rule" originates in their experience of amae.

life may be transferred to the broader community. The
system of duties and obligations which gives expression
to those needs links the individual to parents and
Emperor alike in an affective and hierarchical relationship. This unique relationship of mutual dependency
makes possible the characteristic of Japanese political
culture known as gekokujo, or "rule of the higher by
the lower;"[1] it is especially significant in its operation within the locus of authority in Japanese politics,
the group. This chapter explores the reciprocal nature
of amae.

A. Mutual Dependency in Mother-Child Relationship

The dependency which is encouraged in the child
by the mother's nurturance and indulgence is not the
only dependency which is fostered in the mother-child
relationship. The mother as well develops a dependency
upon her child. This reciprocal dependency finds
expression in different ways at different periods in the
relationship.

To begin with, the Japanese house-wife finds companionship in her small child. Although, as noted in
the previous chapter, their interaction is not primarily
vocal, some verbal exchanges are of course made, and

_____

[1]Maruyama, p. 113.

increasingly so with the age of the child. The result
of the increasing amount of time available to the urban
Japanese housewife is that the mother develops a strong
bond of mutual dependency with the child.[1]

1. Asymmetry of _Amae_ Reciprocity

In the early mother-child relationship, emotional
needs on the part of the infant are being filled in far
greater measure than the mother's; and, certainly, the
infant's needs are much the greater. The emotional
gains to the mother in this symbiotic relationship are
for several years in small and indirect fulfillment
only of her _amae_. At first, for example, a dependency
at the most simple level may be seen in the mother's
need for companionship for which, in return, she provides needed care for the child. To the extent that
amae is reciprocal at this stage, the reciprocity is
indeed "asymmetrical."

Takie Lebra has discussed the asymmetry in some
Japanese social relationships, particularly in relation
to the concept of _on_.[2] Following Doi's approach, she
analyzes _amaeru_ as a component of _on_ and distinguishes
two needs that are both important in the personal

---

[1]Vogel, p. 230. Vogel notes that the Japanese
husband--and the salaryman especially--spends much time
at work and in work-based socializing. Accordingly, the
Japanese wife spends more time at home alone than her
American counterpart.

[2]Lebra, pp. 192-207.

relations among Japanese: to be dependent, and to be depended upon by others.[1] The emotional gains of amaeru, therefore, are reciprocated by the gains of amayakasu, or being amai, --by being depended upon. As the mother-child relationship develops, it embodies more and more this reciprocal nature of amae, in which the mutual dependency of mother and child becomes deeper. Befu explains, "The mother in time begins to seek satisfaction of her emotional needs through her child's dependence on her."[2] This characteristic of the relationship is an enduring one, and is assured by the mother's encouragement of dependency in the child.

        2. Guilt and Achievement Motivation

        As a child grows older, communicates in the language and learns by instruction, the mother's involvement with him acquires new characteristics. In stronger and more direct ways, the mother will be inculcating in him her own values, or the values which she thinks the child should acquire. In Japan, as in any culture, this is a process of creating internal control in the individual. But in Japan, the effectiveness with which amae is inculcated--indeed, the forcefulness with which

---

[1]Ibid., p. 199.

[2]Befu, p. 161.

the mother imposes dependency upon the child--is largely due to her heavy dependence upon him for gratification of her own needs.[1] A third stage of maternal dependency is that in which the mother's emotional needs will be gratified only by evidence that the child has incorporated her values as his own. The Japanese mother, in other words, whose formal position in both the family and society as a whole is one of quiescence and supportiveness, often looks for her self-worth (submerged as it is in the family identity) in the acceptance by her child--especially a son--of the values and behavior which she feels are proper. Primary among these is filial piety.

Still later in life, the mother hopes to find her self-validation in the social successes and professional accomplishments of her child. This phenomenon is more than simply "vicarious gratification";[2] it is an expression of dependency which, by the strength of its demands, compensates with a vengeance for whatever "asymmetry" may have existed in the reciprocal mother-child relationship in its early stages.

---

[1]This emotional need is today quite different from the very practical need in traditional times to have offspring who could be depended upon to care for their aging parents.

[2]Lebra, p. 200.

The Japanese mother expects performance from her
child in satisfaction of her own ego needs. In the
case of a son, a dominant mother may maintain her nurturant control over him as a masculine extension of her
own ego. In such extreme cases, competition between
mother and daughter-in-law of the most bitter sort is
experienced. It is within this dependent relationship
that DeVos finds the source of the Japanese "achievement
motivation;" and it is here also that he determines
guilt to be of greater significance than shame to Japanese social behavior.[1]

Japanese mothers can successfully induce guilt-
motivated behavior (i.e., achievement-oriented behavior)
in a number of ways. All are derived from the emotional
content of the unique mother-child relationship. In the
first instance, a mother may remind her child of all the
sacrifices which she (the family) has made to indulge
him and to provide him with all the opportunities to
make the best of himself. This sort of inducement, conceived in terms of filial piety, is offered and received
in full consciousness and is little more subtle than
what might be said in a similar transaction in the
United States.

---

[1]DeVos, p. 47.

This "achievement motivation" differs from corresponding status seeking in the west in several
aspects. First, mothers in Japan can point to considerably more energy expended over the time from the
child's earliest school years in assisting him with
homework preparation and studies.[1] Second, American
parents may pressure their child to "make good;" but a
child's pursuit of independently defined goals would
not be a cause for social embarrassment. Among Japanese
however, the family's status is very much dependent
upon the success of the new generation. And because
the reciprocity of amae in the family has been institutionalized in the social stress upon filial piety, any
evidence that its mandates have been neglected is perceived as bringing dishonor. This shame reflects not
just on the individual, but on the family as a whole.
This is the second manner in which guilt may be
developed in the mother-child relationship.

The emotional content of the first sort of motivation, based around demands for performance and filial
piety, has more commonly been explained in terms of

_____

[1]The typology of the "kyo-iku mama" is reknown as
a reflection of the valuation upon academic achievement,
of the competitiveness in admission to superior schools
at all levels of education above primary, and of the
social and familial pressures on the young person to succeed in the examinations which are the critical factors
in determining his life-long career, and therefore,
social options.

on-giri; the latter, which springs from a concern about
the reactions of others to one's behavior, in terms of
shame. A closer look at these two concepts will show
their relationships to guilt and will support amae as
the emotion actually underlying both kinds of motivation.

3. The Amae Element in On-giri-ninjo

For many years on has best been understood as a
benevolent act whose performance creates an intangible
debt which the recipient is duty-bound to honor, if not
actually repay. In the case of parents, a child must
never forget his duty toward them, but repayment of the
accumulated favors, instruction, indulgences, and
sacrifices made in bringing the child up--much less in
bringing him into the world--cannot be made in a
lifetime. The nature of on in relationships outside the
family is such that its receipt by one person completely
changes the nature of his relationship with the person
who has done the kindness. Jugaku characterizes the
change as one which transforms the two people involved
from tanin (strangers) into two who will newly perceive
each other in a way approximating "him and none other."[1]
To establish a friendship is a step not lightly

---

[1]Jugaku Akiko, Characteristics of Japanese People
Seen in the Peculiarities of Japanese Language (Tokyo:
Association of International Education, 1970), p. 33.

undertaken, because to ask and receive a favor carries
with it a burden of honor which may be retained throughout life. Perhaps most important to note is the fact
that an on not only creates, in turn, an obligation to
repay the kindness (giri), but it creates as well a
justified expectation on the part of the recipient that
further kindnesses may be sought and received. The continuing social obligations placed on the on-giver, then,
are every bit as great as those on the giri-holder.[1]

In the past, the network of debts and obligations
expressed in on-giri has been emphasized; and its impact
has been found primarily in the rigid social requisites
built around the mechanics of fulfilling duties. The
operation of on-giri within the hierarchical relationships usually characterized as oyabun-kobun ("father-role
--child-role") was accepted as a value in and of itself,
embodying the benevolence of paternalism. Only recently
has it been recognized that "indulgence by the socially
inferior in the superior's affective discharge is an
essential ingredient of the on relationship."[2] This
indulgence in the oya-ko relationship is commonly
referred to as ninjo ("human feelings"). Although the

---

[1]For my understanding of this aspect of on
(necessarily still incomplete), I am indebted to
Professor L. W. Beer.

[2]Befu, p. 161.

reciprocity of giri (in this sense, "duty") and ninjo is not a new discovery, Doi has shown the inseparability of the two owing to their common roots in amae. For Doi, ninjo means specifically "knowing how to amaeru properly and how to respond to the call of amaeru in others."[1] Giri serves to bind people in amae relation- ships.[2]

In any relationship between two people as people, a Japanese hopes to have his dependency needs gratified; he hopes to be the beneficiary of ninjo; he hopes to be able to amaeru. The role of giri in personal relation- ships is to restrain amaeru behavior which might other- wise know no bounds. As such, the mechanisms of on-giri represent formalized behavior patterns which insure that amae needs will be met, but never with the total self-indulgence that might be sought. The actual opera- tion of these patterns will be made clearer in the con- text of later chapters.

It is easy to understand how the operation of on-giri might be viewed mechanistically by Benedict and others. Their perception of a "shame" culture is one in

---

[1]Doi Takeo, "Giri-Ninjo: An Interpretation," Aspects of Social Change in Modern Japan, Ronald P. Dore, ed. (Princeton: Princeton University Press, 1967), p. 328.

[2]Ibid., p. 333.

which the socially approved patterns must be upheld only
to avoid ostracism:

> A man is shamed either by being openly ridiculed
> and rejected or by fantasying to himself that he
> has been made ridiculous.... So long as his bad
> behavior does not "get out into the world" he
> need not be troubled and confession appears to
> him merely a way of courting trouble.[1]

But what Doi and others like DeVos after him
have understood is that the value of _amae_ _is_ internalized
in the Japanese--largely through the child-rearing
approach described above, and that guilt is just as
important a motivation to Japanese behavior as is fear
of shame, if not more so. In fact, insofar as shame
was thought to arise from the disgrace which is brought
upon those around you, the source of guilt is clearly in
not having fulfilled one's duties to them.

   4. Conclusion

Whether fear of external ostracism or avoidance
of internal anxiety is the actual psychological mechan-
ism assuring acceptable behavior in general, both
incentives are created within the dependency orientation
developed in the Japanese. But in the case of the
"achievement motivation" in particular as found by DeVos
and others, guilt stands alone as the psychological
explanation. Befu summarizes this explanation very
clearly:[2]

---

[1]Benedict, pp. 222-224.   [2]Befu, pp. 161-162.

As the child develops dependence on the mother's
discharge of affect, the mother in turn begins
to seek satisfaction of her emotional needs
through her child's dependence on her. The
child's attempt to act contrary to the mother's
desire (and thus act independently) tends to
provoke anxiety in the mother, since she is thus
no longer needed and can no longer satisfy her
emotional needs. The mother's anxiety and consequent suffering in turn, when communicated to
the child through the devious means through
which emotion is communicated, is likely to
cause the child to feel guilty and attempt to
correct the situation... In other words, parental
suffering tends to be interpreted by the child as
a result of his failure, and because the child
does not like to see his parents--the sources of
his emotional gratification--suffer, he tries
to relieve parental suffering by conforming to
parental wishes. To the extent that parents
wish for their children's success and achievement
in his world, these parental wishes serve as a
powerful source of motivation to achieve success.

What has been shown is that in muted fashion, the
mother creates guilt in fundamentally the only way she
can, namely, by demanding to be indulged in the mutual
dependency of the mother-son relationship. By encouraging the child to amaeru in a period of prolonged nurturance and indulgence, the Japanese mother insures that
when the time comes, her own amae needs will be met.

B. Amae and Authority: Reciprocity of Obedience and
    Indulgence

George DeVos has introduced a new element in the
reciprocal content of amae in the mother-child relationship: by identifying obedience as the reciprocal of

being indulged, he suggests very forcefully the sig-

nificance of _amae_ to Japanese politics:

> /The Japanese child7 is encouraged to be _sunao_,
> or obedient. In this context of dependency the
> Japanese also develop a capacity, by passive
> means, to induce nurturant behavior toward them-
> selves by other. The inductive manipulation of
> others to secure care for oneself is expressed in
> the Japanese word _amae_.... Japanese mothers are
> conscious that, in order to maintain compliance
> and obedience, they must satisfy the feelings of
> dependency developed within an intense mother-
> child relationship. Goodwill must be maintained
> so that the child will willingly undertake the
> increasingly heavy requirements and obligations
> placed upon him in the school and the home.
> There is a direct cultural linkage between con-
> tentment and compliance.[1]

We turn now to key respects in which the mother's

role in the family--in relation to both children and

husband--embodies this reciprocity between obedience and

indulgence, and perpetuates a culture-wide set of atti-

tudes toward authority in general.

1. Mother and Father: Authority Relations in

    the Family

The nature of the relationship between the mother

and father themselves is significant to authority rela-

tions inside the Japanese family. As we have seen, it

is the mother who has the greater contact with the

---

[1]DeVos, p. 47. Interestingly, Vogel translates
sunao to mean "gentle." This coincidence of "obedience"
and "gentleness" suggests that the passivity encouraged
in the young as part of _amae_ enjoys some social sanction
in and of itself; it also conveys a last meaning for
"sunao": "submissive."

child; it is the mother who gratifies most of the
expressed needs of the child. Likewise, it is she who
most often disciplines the child when necessary, (although threat of punishment at the hands of the more
severe father is used sometimes by a despairing mother).
As the Norbecks make clear, children soon learn that
the words of the more indulgent mother may sometimes go
ignored--and often without pain of punishment, but that
"those of the father must ordinarily be heeded." It is
clear from their description that the child's understanding of family relations is that the authority of
the father is greater than the mother's: "The words and
actions of the father carry more weight than those of
others...."[1]

Although the nature of authority is clearer in the
case of the vertical parent-child relationship (which,
as Nakane notes, is the more important family link),[2] the
nature of the relationship between husband and wife is
more important for understanding the amae basis of control in the family.

---

[1]Norbeck, p. 660.

[2]Nakane Chie, Japanese Society (Berkeley: Unisity of California Press, 1970), p. 128. Fukutake
states explicitly: "The central relation within the
family is not the relationship between husband and wife,
but the relationship between parents and children."
Fukutake Tadashi, Japanese Rural Society (London: Cornell University Press, 1972), R. P. Dore, trans., p. 39.

Pragmatically, responsibility for the daily business of maintaining the household, raising the children, and managing the family finances rests with the Japanese wife. According to Vogel,[1] married life in many cases is a muted and patiently undertaken process of adjustment in which accommodation (mostly on the part of the wife) is made not so much to individual personalities involved as to the prescribed roles in marriage:

> Mamachi families solidly dislike extended mutual exploration of emotion, particularly the more primitive sentiments of love and hate, and consider it best for each to control his feelings and to limit his expression of personal demands.[2]

Overtness is not a characteristic of Japanese interpersonal communication in the first place; it appears to be even less so in the case of husband-and-wife discussions. Vogel stresses that among Japanese wives, there exists no sense "that they can achieve as much by open expression of opinion as they can by subtle manipulation."[3]

Such "husband management" takes any number of forms, such as planting an idea in the husband's mind and then allowing him to take credit for the idea himself, or instructing a child, whom the father is loathe to refuse, to make the request which the mother wants.[4]

---

[1]Vogel, p. 175ff. [2]Ibid., p. 196. [3]Ibid.

[4]For colorful examples of such "husband management," see Vogel, pp. 200-203.

The marriage relationship is one in which we may
expect to find clear examples of amaeru, which can be a
particularly potent form of manipulation. As in the
example drawn from Natsume's novel,[1] a woman may actively
amaeru, or passively endear herself in a childish way
that invites the husband's indulgence and that will win
his assent to her wishes. Although men may also amaeru
within family relationships, it is more noticeable--and
acknowledged--in the behavior of women, for reasons
which Beardsley presents:

> Women's inclination toward dependency is more
> difficult to assess without specific psycholo-
> gical evidence because their social roles are
> institutionalized with little tolerance for
> dependency. Within the family, most girls are
> expected to care for their own needs early and
> to discipline themselves against intruding on the
> prerogatives of others. In adulthood and outside
> the family, they must be largely self-reliant,
> in addition to learning how to exert indirect
> pressures and win others over by emotional warmth,
> if they are to have their way. The very fact
> that women are given so little scope for
> institutionalized dependency perhaps accounts for
> their reliance on amae, in the sense of cozening
> and wheedling or being lovable enough to be
> granted favors which they cannot demand on equal
> terms with boys. Hence, the Japanese themselves
> associate amae with women.[2]

The manipulative skills of the Japanese wife,
however, are not limited to particular issues in family

---

[1]Supra., p. 37.   [2]Beardsley, p. 378.

life, but are in fact inherent in her position of control in the family, and especially in relation to her raising the children. Although that is a position of control, it is in important respects a position of dependency. Amae makes the bridge between the two positions: "Control from a seemingly dependent position is the heart of amae."[1]

Vogel writes:[2]

> The techniques by which the mother builds a close relationship with the children may be viewed as a brilliant adaptation to the problem of managing the children without a clear mandate of authority that would permit her to exercise more direct sanctions.

These techniques whose functions Vogel comprehends are the child-rearing practices embodying amae. What we find in the Japanese family, then, is authority resting with the head of the family, the father/husband. For all intents and purposes, however, decisions in the family are made by the mother/wife. This she achieves not only by amaeru in the active, coquettish sense, but by fostering amae in its more pervasive, passive-manipulative sense. "The Mamachi wife...in some ways treats her husband as her eldest child. As in dealing with her child, she tries to keep him continuously

---

[1]DeVos, p. 453.   [2]Vogel, p. 251.

happy and satisfied, because then he will respond automatically to her wishes."[1]

In the absence of any real delegation of author- ity by her husband, the Japanese mother maintains her operative control over the children by indulging them. She manages her children--as well as her husband (and thus maintains the appearance of her authority)--by gaining their compliance in exchange for assuring their contentment. By encouraging her family to be emotion- ally dependent upon her, she is able to achieve power in a position which is formally dependent upon her husband.[2]

The authority relations within the Japanese family present clear prototypes of Japanese political relations which have been widely classified as "rule from below."

2. Rule from Below: Patterns in Traditional Japanese Politics

Maruyama Masao has characterized three person- ality types in Japanese politics whose relationship exemplifies the separation of power from authority. The "Portable Shrine," whose position is the highest of

---

[1]Ibid., p. 200.

[2]Viewed within the patriarchical hierarchy of traditional Japanese kinship, she is subordinate to her sons as well.

the three in the national hierarchy and who is vested
legally with the greatest power, represents authority.
In actuality, however, he is often little more than a
robot whose largest contribution to the conduct of politics is in "doing nothing" (i.e., legitimizing the power
that is wielded elsewhere). The "Official" actually ex-
ercises the power in the system. His rule is built upon
the legitimacy passing down from the "Shrine," which the
official attentively "holds aloft." The third figure is
the "Outlaw," whose function is to prod the official to
take action, usually accomplished by violence or by the
threat of it.[1]

---

[1]Maruyama, pp. 128-129. Maruyama has described
the roles, and the "system of irresponsibilities" which
they comprise, quite clearly in the context of Japan's
pre-war military rule only. Accordingly, Maruyama
presents these characteristics as aberrations; the norm,
in this context, is "democracy:" "The principle known
as 'rule of the higher by the lower' is, in effect, an
irrational explosion of irresponsible, anonymous power,
and can occur only in a society in which power from
below is not officially recognized. It is, so to speak,
an inverted form of democracy" (p. 113).
        Chalmers Johnson, however, finds these roles
embodied in all periods of Japanese politics:

> Maruyama's tripod also seems to live on into
> the present... /Nagai Yonosuke7 suggests that
> today the Portable Shrine is the Liberal
> Democratic Party (LDP) faction leader, held aloft
> by the bureaucracy, and prodded by the new ronin
> --the press, and, he might have added, the
> emerging forces of consumer protest, residents'
> committees, and "reform" (kakushin) mayors.

/Chalmers Johnson, "Japan: Who Governs? An
Essay on Official Bureaucracy." Journal of Japanese
Studies 2, No. 1 (Autumn 1975), p. 1. Johnson cites
Nagai Yonosuke, "Social and External Factors Influencing
Japanese Foreign Policies during the 1970's." Unpub-
lished paper for the Japan Institute of International
Affairs and the International Institute for Strategic
Studies.7

Traditionally, of course, and for most of Japan's history, the source of legitimacy in government has been the blessings of the Emperor. The Emperor's authority has not always been political; rather, for the most part, it was religious and ethical in nature.

The mythology promulgated even before the earliest known rulers of Yamato--used, presumably, by leaders seeking to justify the primacy of their own clan (uji)-- established the divine lineage of the Emperor from the Sun Goddess Amaterasu. To this day the perpetuation of the imperial line has maintained the special relation- ship which members of the Japanese heritage feel for their spiritual inheritance; and if not until this day, at least until the discrediting of State Shinto after World War II, the protection of imperial rule has assured that government over Japan would be in accordance with the benevolent terms of that special relationship.

The terms of that relationship have been inter- preted variously at different periods in history in the light of Confucianist, Buddhist, and nationalist beliefs. But in all periods, these interpretations have been offered by pretenders to and defenders of power to enhance the legitimacy of their particular claims to represent the authority of the Emperor.

Japanese history reveals few instances of active rule by a member of the imperial family. It is at once

ironical and instructive that the act of greatest
decisiveness and impact taken by any Emperor was the same
announcement which foretold the end of the imperial institution as the Portable Shrine in Japanese politics: the
surrender proclamation of Emperor Hirohito on August 15,
1945.[1]

It is important to note, however, that even at those
times when the Emperor was furthest removed from the seat
of de facto rule in the country,[2] his rightful position

---

[1]See "Imperial Rescript on the End of the War,"
Sources in Modern East Asian History and Politics, Theodore McNelly, ed. (New York: Appleton-Century-Crofts,
1967), pp. 169-170. The Emperor's repudiation of any
divine attributes was subsequently made on January 1, 1946.

[2]The first clear example of the gap between the
formal seat of imperial power and the actual exercise of
power was in the Heian period (794-1185) during which the
Fujiwara family succeeded in establishing its hegemony in
the court at Heiankyo. The family's control was won not
simply by gaining important official posts, but more significantly, by intermarrying repeatedly with the imperial
family. By wedding their daughters to successive Emperors,
the men of Fujiwara were able over several generations to
exercise direct control through the institution of a
regency. As soon as a son were born to an Emperor, the
Fujiwara's would have him abdicate in favor of the young
heir, thereby perpetuating the regency, whose power was
exercised by the maternal Fujiwara grandfathers and uncles.
The kamakura bakufu was a military government
headed by a Shogun who ruled from the town of Kamakura in
the name of the Imperial court which was in Kyoto. Continuous from the Heian period discussed above, a regent
presided over the court in behalf of a child Emperor,
while the abdicated Emperor engaged in court intrigue and
employed what few ceremonial powers he still retained to
his best advantage, from his "cloistered" position. But
during the Kamakura period, not only was an Imperial
regency established, but the Hojo regency established
itself over a figurehead Shogun, thus creating a new position of political power, fully four steps removed from
the cloistered Emperor.
/For a full history of the Hojo Regency, see George
B. Sansom, A History of Japan to 1334 (Stanford:

as head of state, such as it was conceived at the time, was never questioned. Not only were the Japanese people dependent upon the Emperor in an emotional sense for their spiritual sense of identity, but so also were the court nobles and military officials dependent upon him in a political sense for the legitimacy of their rule.[1]

3. Politicization of Emperor's Role

With the fragmentation of clan strength and the consolidation of power in the centralized bakufu (military government) accomplished by the Tokugawa Shogunate (1603-1867), competition for imperial favors among warlords declined, and along with it, the opportunity for the Imperial House to interject into political affairs. Tokugawa family interests were well defended, but protected at the expense of national isolation and stagnation. It was only with the forceful arrival of foreign visitors, beginning with Commodore Perry, and the irresistible introduction of western influences that the stability of almost 250 years was shaken.

The role of the Emperor became a focal issue in the political dialogue that preceded the "Restoration

---

Stanford University Press, 1958), pp. 371-385. For a detailed account of its internecine complexities, see pp. 409-413. Also Mikiso Hane, Japan: A Historical Survey (New York: Charles Scribner's Sons, 1972), pp. 53ff._/

[1]Sansom, p. 377.

of Imperial Rule" in 1868. And the ideology of the Meiji

Restoration linked more forcefully than ever before the

loyalty, duty, and spiritual indebtedness toward the

family and those same obligations toward the Emperor.

The results of that linkage was a new national conscious-

ness.[1] Hindsight allows us to see also that the success

of the Meiji leaders (genro) in harnessing the energies

of a new nationalism was assisted by the cultural pro-

pensities among Japanese, and significantly among them,

to amaeru.

Over the years preceding 1868, the political

implications of the slogan sonno ("revere the Emperor")[2]

were alternately supportive and subversive of the

Tokugawa regime. Finally, under the leadership of dis-

illusioned and disenfranchised lower samurai from the

distant han (provinces) of Satsuma and Choshu,[3] military

---

[1]Maruyama Masao, Studies in the Intellectual History of Tokugawa Japan (Tokyo: University of Tokyo Press,
1974), Mikiso Hane, trans., p. 343.

[2]The incapacity of the self-indulgent and financi-
ally over-extended Tokugawa administration to defend the
country against the demands of western expansion was
quickly apparent to a majority of court officials and
samurai around the country, many of whom agreed that the
lesson of the earlier, Chinese experience was that Japan
must increase the central, national power to meet the
external challenge. "The search for an agent in whom
this centralized political authority could ultimately be
lodged brought the doctrine of sonno to the political
forefront." Ibid., p. 363.

[3]For a general description of the anti-bakufu
leadership of the Satsuma and Choshu han, see Hane,
pp. 256-266.

pressure was brought to bear against the bakufu so that anti-bakufu leaders in Edo were able to convince the Shogun to voluntarily "restore" rule to the newly ascended Emperor Meiji.[1]

Loyalty to the Emperor was unquestionably a motivation on the part of many of the ambitious samurai who took direction of Japan's crisis effort. And if the political reforms away from the "feudalism" of the Tokugawa were not toward liberal democratic government, they were certainly in the direction of a strengthened monarchy. But the Emperor Meiji was young; and for the genro who directed the nation-building known as the Meiji Restoration, the Emperor's primary role was undoubtedly in overcoming the disadvantage of there

---

[1]Certainly the relatively egalitarian ruling principle of ikkun banmin ("one prince, all the people") stood in great contrast to the exploitative "divide and rule" approach employed so effectively by Ieyasu and his descendants. The fact that Sansom /A History of Japan 1615 to 1867 (Stanford: Stanford University Press, 1963), p. 242./ concludes his study of Japanese history with "and in 1867 the rule of the throne is fully restored," indicated how far removed the Emperor had been from the locus of power until that time. But to speak of a return to direct Imperial rule overstates the case. Nevertheless, James W. White states, "In 1868 the Tokugawa regime was overthrown and the Meiji Emperor was 'restored' to direct rule." "State Building and Modernization: The Meiji Restoration," in Crisis, Choice, and Change: Historical Studies of Political Development. Gabriel Almond, Scott Flanagan, and Robert Mundt, eds.; (Boston: Little, Brown and Co., 1973), p. 500.

having been no popular participation in the revolutionary process of change, by achieving what Fukuzawa
Yukichi called "the implantation of the concept of
'nation' in the minds of the people of the entire
country."[1] The Japanese concept of nation thus took the
form of the family-state system, and incorporated
emperor worship as its expression.

C. The Family-State System

Nakamura finds the linkage between family and
state in the Japanese devotion to a specific individual
as a concrete expression of a social unit--and, more
importantly, of the social values inherent in that unit.

> The family in ancient Japan was not an abstract
> concept, but was embodied in the person of the
> living family head. There is also a tendency to
> identify...the Emperor with the state.... (Such a
> term as "family-state"...would have been
> rejected by westerners as self-contradictory.
> The Japanese, however, felt no inconsistency in
> the term, but found it good and valid.)[2]

The Japanese term for household, ie, carries an
abundance of meanings. Fukutake stresses the following
meaning, perhaps most significant for the rural communities which he was studying:

> ...the continuing entity, perpetuated in princi-
> pal by patriarchical descent, from ancestor to
> descendant, an entity of which the family group
> at any one time is only the current concrete
> manifestation.[3]

---

[1]Quoted by Maruyama (1974), p. 367.
[2]Nakamura, p. 448-449. [3]Fukutake, p. 39.

Ishida even finds a normative connotation to the term: "a set of values about how members were to behave."[1]

Ishida goes on to portray the paternalism which operated within the hierarchical structure of the _ie_ and which gives the _ie_ its four features:[2]

1. The _ie_ is an extended family with hierarchical relations among the branches.

2. Each family is patriarchical in structure.

3. Members of each family owed obedience to the head of that family; correspondingly, branch families owed obedience to the stem family. In return, the family head provided security for family members; likewise, the main family offered 'social security' for the branch families, notably in times of need.

4. The solidarity of the _ie_ was the ideological basis for the family-state concept, which conceived of the state as a single family with the Emperor at its head, creating a relationship between subject and ruler which institutionalizes the same values as exist in that between father and son.

1. Traditional Political Values: Linkage
       Between _Ie_ and _Kokutai_

For Ishida, the most significant value operating in the above context is filial piety, or obedience,

-----

[1]Ishida Takeshi, _Japanese Society_ (New York: Random House, 1971), p. 49.
       [2]_Ibid_.

loyalty, and proper attention to the duties incumbent
upon a son--and by extension, a subject. The distinction between those two roles (son and subject) was further de-emphasized by an organic concept of the Japanese family-state, originating in the myth of the
heavenly origins of the Japanese islands. Because the
Emperor provided the link between the heavens and man on
earth, each Japanese was "intrinsically dependent" upon
the Emperor. Conversely, as a symbol of the familistic
unity of the Japanese people, the Emperor was bound to
his people. Neither the Emperor nor the people could
be conceived of as standing apart from the other. In
this respect, the Emperor stood in the same position as
a household head, as described by Nakane:

> Although the power of each individual household
> head is often regarded as exclusively his own, in
> fact it is the social group, the "household,"
> which has the ultimate integrating power, a power
> which restricts each member's behavior and
> thought, including that of the household head
> himself.[1]

So just as with the household head and the _ie_,
the Emperor and his people were bound together in a
relationship of mutual dependency in a very fundamental
sense.

----

[1]Nakane, p. 14.

2. Emperor Veneration

If, as the saying went, "your parents' on is deeper than the seas and higher than the mountains," it was but a short step to the realization that one's debt to the Emperor was even greater. This step was encouraged by the implementation by the Meiji leaders of a program of compulsory education, whose content stressed the moral imperatives of being Japanese--of being a member of the Japanese nation, and of being a subject of the Emperor who stood as the head of the patriarchical Japanese family-state.

> Our nation is, as it were, one family, of which the Emperor is the head or patriarch, and this relation has subsisted from the first foundation of our Empire down to the present time. Never, during the whole long period of our history, has there been a single instance of a subject presuming to attempt to place himself on the throne, and never have we been conquered by a foreign invader. This relation between the Imperial House and the people, I repeat, is the most important factor in the development of our national character, and, as stated in the Rescript, is the basis of our education.[1]

The inculcation of this new nationalism was facilitated by what Nakamura identifies as the Japanese way of thinking:

> The Japanese way of thinking, which pays the highest respect to some particular living person

---

[1]Baron Kikuci Dairoku, Japanese Education, (London: John Murrary, 1909); cited in Robert King Hall, Shūshin: The Ethics of a Defeated Nation (New York: Columbia University Press, 1949), pp. 54-55.

and at the same time bows down to hierarchical
distinctions of social status, culminates in
ascribing absolutely divine attributes to the
individual at the top of the hierarchy of Japanese society. Emperor worship is thus established.[1]

Although the role of the Emperor was certainly

politicized during this period to a greater degree than

ever before, his role was more important as a symbol of

the natural bond which has always existed between Japa-

nese religion and nation.[2] By joining religious rites

and civil administration--affect and control--fully

together in Emperor worship, the energies of emotional

dependency and the ethics of personal behavior which

channel those energies became fully institutionalized

in the political realm.

D. Dependency as the Basis for Authority

From an understanding of the mutual dependency of

leader and follower comes the recognition that control

is not exercised in one direction only. Controls are

---

[1]Nakamura, p. 467. Although the expression
"Emperor worship" has been used in English, there is no
element of deism in the Japanese religious consciousness.
Even if the living Emperor were deemed to have embodied
the spiritual essence of kami (objects of reverence and
celebration in the syncretic belief system of the Japanese), the term "veneration" would better represent the
devotion of the Emperor's subjects than "worship."

[2]H. Byron Earhardt, Japanese Religion: Unity and
Diversity (Encino, California: Dickenson Publishing
Co., Inc., 1974), p. 8.

felt on every individual in Japanese society, regardless
of his place in the social hierarchy. The following
chapter will examine the group as the locus of authority
in Japanese life and will detail the manner in which '
control is maintained. In ending this chapter, however,
I should like to draw some conclusions about amae and
Japanese attitudes toward authority.

1. "Lack of Self"

As a result of American war-time experience with
"fanatical" Japanese suicide missions and kamikaze
pilots, and from post-war studies of the sort summarized
in the preceding chapter, a clear picture of the Japanese has emerged in our minds which includes no sense of
"selfhood." Many Japanese appear to be concurring in
this self-characterization, and it is prominent in Doi's
diagnosis of Japan's social ills.[1] But from the beginning it is wise to take heed of Befu's caution:[2]

> We /Americans/ feel that each individual should
> examine, personally decide on, and remain con-
> sistent with a set of coherent and logical prin-
> ciples, and when the Japanese do not emphasize
> these things, we are likely to seek explanations
> in terms of some concept like their underdeveloped
> sense of self. This, however, tells us more about
> our own understanding of self and personhood than
> it tells us about the Japanese.

The nature of Japanese selfhood is closely
related to amae. As has been shown, individualism and

---

[1]Doi (1973), pp. 132-141.   [2]Befu, p. 60.

values of autonomy are not inculcated in Japanese children; belongingness and dependency are. It has become
a truism that the individual in Japanese society finds
his identity through membership in his primary group.[1]
One can observe the great difference between the vitality
of the Japanese in group interaction and his "dead-ness"
alone; and this difference reflects the sense of
nothingness that the Japanese has about himself.[2] It is
through amae that the individual affirms his self-
identity. Because it is only by his participation in
the social group that he can overcome his "lack of
self," he abandons his autonomous self (nothingness) and
asserts his dependent self (amaeru) to be a member of
the group and to establish his selfhood. Doi makes this
relationship clear: "man cannot possess a self without
previous experience of amaeru."[3]

2. "Authoritarianism"

An inadequate understanding in the past of Japanese "selfhood" has led many to conclude that the

---

[1]As Doi (1973) humorously puts it, "they will
usually put up with anything in order to belong to a
group (p. 138).

[2]The psychological sense of "nothingness" that
comes from being outside the human circle of amae is
presented even more poignantly to the Japanese because
of eastern philosophical notions of "nothingness" that
impart a metaphysical reality to the expereince as well.
Conversation with Professor L. W. Beer, April 28, 1976.

[3]Doi (1973), p. 139.

Japanese national character is "authoritarian,"[1] by
which we mean unquestioning obedience and submissiveness
to the commands of those "in authority" (read "power").[2]
Even scholars like Befu contribute to the misunder-
standing with statements like, "the indulgent,
non-authoritarian child-rearing practices of Japanese
lead to an adult personality in which submissiveness to
authority is a salient characteristic."[3]

Most simply, submissiveness is seen as arising
from the "lack of self;" even with a bit more sophistication, we continue to find individual submissiveness
being shown to the group which has become the source of
a sense of self. But both conclusions overlook the fact
that submissiveness (sunao) among Japanese is mitigated,
balanced, reciprocated by indulgence of amaeru. DeVos
presents the reciprocity between the two in these words:[4]

> A sunao person maintains basic trust in authority
> and finds it easy and natural to follow directives
> of others with the implicit assumption that he
> will be taken care of should special needs arise.

---

[1]In this respect, Benedict helped us to believe
what we probably wanted to about the Japanese, much as
Theodore W. Adorno, et al., /The Authoritarian Personality (New York: Harper & Row, 1950)/ did in relation to
their Nazi allies in World War II.

[2]Webster's New World Dictionary, Second College
Edition (1974) defines "authoritarian" as follows:
"...characterized by unquestioning obedience to authority,
as that of a dictator, rather than individual freedom of
judgment and action."

[3]Befu, p. 29.   [4]DeVos, p. 48.   Emphasis mine.

The sunao attitude does seem to facilitate a high tolerance level among Japanese for seemingly unrewarded endeavors, such as in a demanding apprentice-ship relationship,[1] or in war. But in fact, the psychological rewards of amae are assured to the sunao individual. And the content of such psychological rewards is precisely the fullest expression of "selfhood" possible in the Japanese understanding of that term ("jibun").

The willingness to have matters taken care of by those in positions of leadership, without feeling the need for mass participation in the process of defining issues and articulating demands, has been viewed by many outside observers as an inherent limitation upon the full realization of democracy in Japan. That this passive attitude does exist today among Japanese is shown in the following statement from a round-table discussion about Japanese economic problems: "/T/he consciousness is very strong among the people that some great leader will deal with the matter and that they

---

[1]See DeVos, "Apprenticeship and Paternalism," Modern Japanese Organization and Decision-Making, Ezra F. Vogel, ed. (Berkeley: University of California Press, 1975); pp. 210-227.

need only to make their own special order."[1] But such an
attitude of trust is clearly different from submissiveness, and the popular expectation of responsiveness to
"their own special order" shows how different the two
are.[2]

---

[1]"Symposium of Strong Points and Weaknesses of
Japanese Economy," Japan Economic Journal, December 30,
1975, p. 11.
    A survey conducted at five year intervals since
1953 suggests that this orientation toward government
may be changing. Unfortunately, the question rather
overstates the issue posed here. "Some people say that
if we get good political leaders, the best way to improve
the country is for the people to leave everything to
them, rather than for the people to discuss things among
themselves. Do you agree with this or disagree?"
Responses were tabulated as follows:

	1953	1958	1963	1968
Agree (Traditional)	43%	35%	29%	30%
Depends on time and leader	9	10	13	11
Disagree (Non-traditional)	38	44	47	51
No such leaders expected	3	2	4	3
Don't know	7	9	7	5

    Perhaps the most telling response is not in agree-
ment or disagreement, but in the consistently small percentage of respondents who expressed any doubt that such
"good leaders" were to be found. Even among those who
showed unwillingness to "leave everything to them," basic
trust is placed in the leadership of the country. Question No. 8.1, "Attitude Toward Authoritarian Government"
from Suzuki Tatsuzo, "A Study of the Japanese National
Character," Nipponzin No Kokumisei (II), Hayaski Chikio
et al., eds. (Tokyo: The Institute of Statistical
Mathematics, 1970); p. 519.

    [2]It is important to note this difference in under-
standing, for example, the success of "administrative
guidance" in Japan. The quasi-legislative power given to
bureaucrats in Japanese regulatory agencies may actually
be far less "authoritarian" than the exercise of narrower
prerogatives by American counterparts. Both are trusted
to act in the public welfare: for the American, at best,
it is a matter of professional integrity; for the Japanese, it is also a matter of personal obligation related

The leadership figure in Japan, especially in
the paternalistic role of oyakata, retains the trust
and obedience of his followers (kokata) by being
responsive to their amaeru--by providing for their
special needs with human warmth and feeling (ninjo).
The duties and restraints which this places on the
leader are considerable. His power in dealing with subordinates is limited not only by their dependency upon
him, but by his dependency upon them as well. As the
following chapter will show, his denial of their amae
would result in the loss of his own ability to amaeru.

---

to the value of amae. (Clearly, this factor would make
a difference in responsiveness to interest groups with
personal access to decision makers; that subject is
beyond the scope of this study.) On the subject of administrative guidance, please see Yamanouchi Kazuo, "Administrative Guidance and the Rule of Law," Law in Japan:
An Annual, 7 (1974), 22-33.

E. Conclusion

The essence of social control in Japan is the reciprocity of amae:[1] amae is the source of authority in Japan, and amae defines the limits of that authority as well. This insight suggests that the idea of authority is entirely secondary in Japan to that of dependency; as shown here, the two concepts relate to the same political behavior. It raises also the possibility that the western theoretical dichotomy between authority and autonomy simply may not be congruent with the Japanese experience. Because of amae, autonomy

[1]Cf. David H. Bayley, "The Future of Social Control in Japan," unpublished, University of Denver, 1976. Bayley evaluates those factors in Japan-of-the-future with the greatest potential impact on the informal system of social control which I have characterized here as amae-based. It is interesting to note that of all sources of social change, Bayley finds women's liberation (from the home and with greater equality of rights in the labor market and at the work-place) to have the greatest single potential.

That potential (however distant) is more fully appreciated in light of amae. The mother, as I have shown, is the primary agent of children's enculturation to the values of amae. Her departure from the home with young children would significantly change, over time, the consensus on those values. In the first place, the mother would not be available to perform those characteristic child-rearing practices which communicate indulgence, nurturance, and inseparability; (and the last would be lost in the case of day care, even if the others were preserved). In the second place, the working woman with an identity outside the family would not be compelled to find her self-worth only through the successes of her children; accordingly, a strong psychological impetus to induce amae in them would be lost. In that way, the very foundation of the present system of social control would be eliminated.

seems to present itself as antithetical to dependency; perhaps this alternative conceptualization has a broader application across a wealth of human experience.

Chapter 3 has shown that, in its operation both in the family and in Japanese society, amae results in mutual dependency. The reciprocity inherent in the oya-ko relationship, expressed in the terms of giri-ninjo, reflects a unique Japanese attitude toward authority. That attitude is dependence with an implicit trust that benevolent attention will be paid by those above to special needs if they should arise. The authority of the group is maintained by its ability to satisfy the amae needs of its members. Finally, the group conformism which appears to outsiders to be self-abnegation is in fact directed toward preserving those human relations in which the individual in Japan can assert and express himself most fully.

The following chapter examines the conduct of those human relations in the group setting.

CHAPTER IV

THE GROUP IN JAPANESE ORGANIZATION AND DECISION-MAKING

A. Introduction

The purpose of this chapter is to review how the
principles of organization and group formation operating in contemporary Japan serve to maintain a social
structure which is compatible with long-standing
emphasis upon the values of loyalty and harmony. This
structure facilitates the consensus-building approach
to Japanese decision-making, whose patterns will be
examined to show that the process, like on-giri, is a
convention which channels the expression of amae.
Groupism results in factionalism, whose persistent
appearance in Japanese politics despite dysfunctional
aspects suggests that the needs of amae form the most
potent incentive for factionalism, and many other
institutionalized patterns of social and political
behavior.

Social science studies of Japan abound with
descriptions of Japanese decision-making processes,[1]
the consensus-building priority in Japanese group
dynamics, often with an eye to its impact on United
States-Japan business relations,[2] and the personal
loyalties on which group formation is based, usually
with reference to strains of "feudalism" or "bossism."[3]
A recent book edited by Vogel has helped to restore
balance to much of the over-simplified and dichotomized
/e.g., traditional ("irrational") vs. modern ("rational")/
views of Japanese organizational behavior.[4]

---

[1]Kiyoaki Tsuji, "Decision-Making in the Japanese
Government: A Study of Ringi-sei," Political Development in Modern Japan, Robert E. Ward, ed., (Princeton:
Princeton University Press, 1968), pp. 457-476. Bernard
S. Silberman, "Bureaucratic Development and the Structure of Decision-Making in the Meiji Period," Journal
of Asian Studies, 27, No. 1 (November, 1967), 81-94; and
Silberman, "Ringi-sei--Traditional Value or Organizational Imperatives in the Japanese Upper Civil Service:
1868-1945," Journal of Asian Studies 32, No. 2 (February, 1973), 251-264.

[2]Herman Kahn, The Emerging Japanese Superstate
(Englewood Cliffs, N.J.: Prentice-Hall, Inc., 1970);
especially pp. 40-47. Frank Gibney, Japan: The Fragile
Superpower (New York: W. W. Norton & Co., Inc., 1975).

[3]John Bennett and Iwao Ishino, Paternalism in the
Japanese Economy (Minneapolis: University of Minnesota
Press, 1963). Gerald L. Curtis, Election Campaigning
Japanese Style (New York: Columbia University Press,
1971).

[4]Ezra F. Vogel, ed., Modern Japanese Organization and Decision-Making (Berkeley: University of
California Press, 1975).

The most recent writings on Japanese society
have consistently discussed amae, usually presented as
a cultural value supporting the particular organizational
characteristic under study. For example, Rohlen recognizes that hierarchical organizations in Japanese
business promote authority based on dependency and its
gratification, as opposed to an authority based
strictly on legalism.[1] Befu has pointed out how Doi's
ideas on the psychology of amae dovetail with the
vertical image of Japanese society presented by
Nakane.[2] And none go further than Beer in making
explicit the vital importance of amae in that hierarchy: "A motive force that permeates this 'vertical
society' (tate shakai) is amae."[3]

---

[1]Thomas P. Rohlen, For Harmony and Strength:
Japanese White Collar Organization in Anthropological
Perspective (Berkeley: University of California Press,
1974). The problems related to the informal, group-
based authority in its relation to the formal, legally-
defined authority in Japanese experience will be
discussed in greater detail in Chapter 6.

[2]Harumi Befu, review article of Rohlen, For
Harmony and Strength (Berkeley: University of
California Press, 1974), Journal of Asian Studies 35,
No. 1 (November, 1975), p. 151.

[3]Lawrence W. Beer, "Freedom of Expression in
Japan with Comparative Reference to the United States,"
Comparative Human Rights, Richard P. Claude, ed.,
(Baltimore: Johns Hopkins University Press, 1976);
Chapter 3.

B. The Bases of Group Formation

1. The Vertical Structure of Japanese Society

Nakane's Japanese Society, although brief,
remains one of the most important studies of Japanese
group formation and organizational principles. Those
principles will be reviewed here because of their significance to amae.

The Japanese group is built upon the hierarchical relationship of oyabun-kobun. "The essential
elements of this relationship are that the kobun
receives benefits or help from his oyabun, such as
assistance in securing employment or promotion, and
advice on the occasion of important decision-making.
The kobun, in turn, is ready to offer his services
whenever the oyabun requires them."[1] The dynamics of
the group are primarily the vertical interactions
between leaders and followers; almost all group
members occupy the place of leader in relation to
some, and follower in relation to another: "Groups
in Japan are formed usually by the multiplication of
a vertical relation between two individuals."[2] This
structure is conveyed by the pyramidal image of

---

[1]Nakane, p. 42.   [2]Ibid., p. 44.

interconnected   figures:

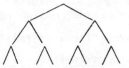

Horizontal relationships may develop within such a
group over time;[1] but full entry into the group is
strictly by means of a primary <u>oya-ko</u> relationship
with a member; and the individual's participation in the
group is regulated by his established relation to a
given group member.[2] Therefore, the individual's
identity with his group is first and foremost through
the concrete personal relationship with a leader; he is
the focal point of group loyalty and dependency.

      2.   The Group as a "Frame"

      A second characteristic of the group in Japan
identified by Nakane is its formation on the basis not
of "attribute" (e.g., learned skills, social status,
level of advancement, and kinship), but of "frame"
(e.g., school, company, ministry). In referring to
their place of work, employees often use the term
"<u>uchi</u>," which means primarily "my home," but by
extension, "my place." That usage is a clear indica-
tion of the degree to which group identity acquired in
the family is transferred to different "frames." This

---

[1]Beer (1976).   [2]Nakane, p. 41.

basis for organization, embracing all levels of the
hierarchy within a "frame," facilitates the primary
modality of oya-ko relations.

The example of contemporary Japanese "paternalism"
most often cited is the characteristic of
labor-management relations which results in the
"enterprise union." The enterprise union illustrates
the organizational principles of "frame," because
unlike its American Federation of Labor counterparts
in the United States, (based on attribute), its
membership includes workers of many skills, rather
than of one craft, and management personnel as well as
employees.[1]

The worker who finds in his workplace his
"uchi" owes loyalty to his "boss" or foreman, who may
have won him the job, if not brought him into the
company as his co-worker in the first place.[2] But
insofar as the worker's group identity is defined by
the enterprise as a whole, personal loyalty is owed
as well up the channels through his boss's boss to the

---

[1]James C. Abegglen, Management and Worker: The
Japanese Solution (Tokyo: Sophia University Press,
1973), p. 85. The C.I.O., with a tradition of
industrial unionism, does organize workers of related
skills in one union, but still on the basis of attribute (e.g., "auto workers").

[2]The labor boss, an intermediary, in effect, between worker and employer is more likely found where employment offered is not permanent. See Bennett and
Ishino.

president of the company. Thus it happens that the positions of individual company unions seldom contradict the goals of the management.

The loyalty of workers to employers is only one half of the reason for harmony between labor and management. Because the rules of amae apply within the group, loyalty is owed as well by employers to their employees.

> Japanese paternalism still derives much of its strength from the traditional expectation that a person playing the role of a boss will assume almost total responsibility for the health and welfare of his workers. The belief that one's boss has a strong feeling of responsibility allows subordinates the complementary expressive feelings of dependence and loyalty toward authority."[1]

Here again, we see that it is the reciprocity of amae that makes it a potent organizational and political force; that is particularly so with respect to consensus-building and factionalism.

C. Consensus-Building: Amae and Emotional Unity in the Group

Group consensus has long been recognized as the basis for decisive action among Japanese. The manner in which they have adapted consensus-building to the

---

[1]DeVos, p. 33.

institutions and processes of parliamentary government
provides the most revealing insights into the
"indigenization" of democratic values in Japan. The
next chapter will analyze the strong emotional content
revealed in the popular reaction against encroachment
on those values. At this point, however, I will show
how leadership and the processes within a group
directed toward achieving consensus and preserving
group unity are conducted in such a way as to permit
and encourage amaeru. Whether one argues that the
group uses amae to achieve its instrumental goals or
that the Japanese seeks out the group to achieve his
own expressive, amae goals, the fact remains that "his
emotional security seems the foremost requisite for a
Japanese engaged in cooperative work."[1]

The nature of that security is the dependency
fostered within the vertical relationships of the
primary group, or amae. Nakane shows that this
security is carefully protected by the work group in
a variety of ways: by developing a strong sense of
"us" against "them;"[2] by promoting a "spirit of love"
for the company;[3] by enforcing a vertical structure in
which the divisive potential of equally competing
powers is avoided;[4] by using a system of life-time

---

[1]Nakane, p. 80.   [2]Ibid., p. 20.
[3]Ibid., p. 19.   [4]Ibid., p. 53.

employment;[1] by building individual social and even
family life around the work group;[2] by employing a style
of leadership in which the function of the leader is
simply to "serve as a pivot for human relations and keep
the peace;"[3] and by deciding issues in a manner which
avoids direct confrontation.[4] According to Nakane, all
these characteristics contribute toward "a cohesive
sense of group unity.../which7 is essential as the
foundation of the individual's total emotional participation in the group."[5] The parallels between the corporation's measures to maintain a harmonious unity and
the family's efforts to promote a nurturant dependency
are unmistakable. The motivation for such "total
emotional participation" is unquestionably amae.

Several of the above characteristics warrant
brief description to show the operation of amae in
these group processes.

1. Life-Time Employment

Certainly the most remarked characteristic of
the Japanese economic structure is the system of
employment which creates "permanent" employees in most

---

[1]Ibid., p. 15.   [2]Ibid., p. 3-4.

[3]Ibid., p. 76.   [4]Ibid., p. 69.

[5]Ibid., p. 19-20.

large enterprises.[1] This is a system of life-time
employment, in which "both the employer and employee
assume that the employment relationship is permanent,
that the company will not discharge or lay off the
employee and that the employee will not change to
another employer during his career."[2] If a worker is
found to be inefficient or even incompetent, once he
has been hired in this manner, a place will be found
for him, and he will be "cared for."

The operation of the seniority system and the
manner of recruitment (i.e., directly from college) are
self-perpetuating and certainly discourage change from
one employer to another. However, the tenacity of the
system, and of employers' commitment to it--even in the
face of economic recession and lowered production[3]--
testifies to its roots in something deeper than the
economic advantage it offered in times of labor

---

[1]Abegglen, pp. 62-74. A principal characteristic of the equally-noted "dual economy" of Japan, however, is the system of "temporary employment" by which
a substantial percentage of the labor force is kept
outside the system described herein. This study
addresses primarily the realm of the "sarariman."

[2]Ibid., p. 24.

[3]Industry in December 1975 was reported as
operating at 25 to 27 percent below capacity. Richard
Halloran, "The Fear is That Hard Times Will Be Permanent," New York Times, February 8, 1976, vi, p. 5.
Unemployment was at its highest rate in sixteen years.

shortage. Impressive also is the commitment of public
funds today in Japan to subsidize the cost borne by
over 27,000 smaller companies who are continuing to
retain and pay "redundant" employees for whom there is
no regular work.[1]

What is in evidence there is government support
for an institution which, although "irrational"[2] in the
minds of foreign economists, is valued for reasons
fully understood only by Japanese.[3] One reason may be
to preserve a system which must be recognized as an
important--if not the most important--channel existing
today for amaeru: submission to a nurturant provider
in a secure life-time relationship of dependency. In
this sense, modern corporations, in addition to

_____

[1]James C. Abegglen, "Japanese Management After
the Storm," The President Directory 1976 (Tokyo: The
Diamond-Time Co., Ltd., 1975); p. 12. Employees kept
at work for only half-days are encouraged to spend the
other half in "civic tasks."

[2]Although the system has a low ability to with-
stand sharp turns in the business cycle, it does offer
several advantages, over and above the identity of
interests of the firm and its employees. They are
1) mobility permitted between jobs within the company,
and, therefore, 2) less restraint on the introduction
of new technology. Ibid.

[3]Public welfare is not comprehensive in Japan,
largely because the paternalistic strains in Japanese
business have made it less necessary than in other indus-
trialized nations. Accordingly, appropriations to subsidize that beneficial activity in depressed periods are
an entirely "rational" alternative to direct government
involvement in increased welfare expenditure.

providing social security in Japan, may be recognized
by decision-makers as the only institution able to
provide something the "rationalized" government seems
unable to provide: "The feeling of allegiance in
respect to the country is being displayed through the
company, that is, in the form of being displayed in
this single route alone."[1]

    2. Company Involvement in Family Life.

Companies are able to be the focus for emotional
involvement not only because of the life-time relationship with its employees, but because of the extent to
which individual lives are increasingly centered
around them. Because the employment relationship is
not contractual, but personal--and as suggested, very
familistic, it is not surprising that the nurturance of
the Japanese work group reaches extensively into the
social and family lives of its members. The employer
or firm shows its responsibility for workers by
willingly contributing to such diverse aspects of
living as education for workers' children, family
budget management, and celebration of religious
ceremonies.[2] Most large corporations provide family

---

[1]"Symposium on Strong Points and Weaknesses of
Japanese Economy," Japan Economic Journal 13, No.679-
680, December 30, 1975; p. 10.

[2]Abegglen (1973), p. 138-141.

housing for many employees, which makes the work group
the center of activities not only for the worker himself, but for his family as well. Increasingly,
activities for wives have been initiated from within the
company also. Family vacations are often enjoyed at
company-leased resort facilities.

A full schedule of social affairs for the work
group insures the worker's identification with the
company as more than a place of work. These ostensibly
voluntary activities are viewed by leaders as essential
to team work and group maintenance because, as Rohlen
points out, "The emotional momentum and sense of group
solidarity are largely cultivated during such social
activities."[1]

The tremendous involvement of the work group in
the affairs of its individual members is quite natural
to begin with, but its effect over time is to increase
the degree to which the worker and even his family
identify with the work group as a unifying and nurturing
whole.

3. Style of Leadership

Leadership as it is commonly thought of in the
United States emphasizes performance abilities

---

[1]Thomas P. Rohlen, "The Company Work Group,"
Modern Japanese Organization and Decision-Making, Ezra
F. Vogel, ed. (Berkeley: University of California
Press, 1975), p. 190.

(e.g., planning) and prescriptive attributes (e.g.,
honesty). In Japan, qualities of leadership are
defined overwhelmingly in terms of personal characteristics. This has been shown in a recent study by Austin:[1]
"Authority is legitimated not by being depersonalized,
but by personalization; not as abstract and cold
equality but as particular and intimate concern. This
is the mark of true leadership in the Japanese organization."[2]

As revealed in the oya-ko relationship, performance is expected more of the followers than of the
leader, who is depended upon for support and security
offered in the spirit of "human feelingness." As the
focal point of the group, the leader provides this
security not only in individual relationships with
subordinates (by "taking them under his wing,"
"opening a pathway for them and guiding them,"
"comforting them when they are troubled," and "pro-
tecting them even when they are at fault"), but by
using his personal attributes (a "big heart," "human-
ness," "the taste of a real person," and an almost
intuitive communication with his men) to assure

---

[1]Lewis Austin, Saints and Samurai: The Political
Cultures of the American and Japanese Elites (New Haven:
Yale University Press, 1975).

[2]Ibid., p. 30.

cooperation and a sense of unity within the group.[1]
Because the able leader recognizes this underlying
unity as the sine qua non of any cooperative endeavor,
his energies will be directed toward maintaining it;
this he does by encouraging amaeru.

The amae nature of the Japanese style of leadership is seen in this instruction from the Self Defense
Force Handbook for NCO's: "Squad leaders must act like
affectionate mothers /to/ their squad members." It is
also revealed in the connection which Austin makes
between the patterns of the business world and the more
overtly emotional style of the gay quarters:[2]

> What one learns from female society is the
> sublety and the intensity of the emotional
> patterns that interweave themselves between and
> under the stoical and formal surface of the male
> bureaucracy. And one learns how to recognize,
> to call up and to use hidden feelings--the fear
> of loneliness, the desire for communion--in the
> service of the organization's goals....

The Study of Japanese National Character
reveals the persistency of the paternalistic style of
leadership; and the analysts' conclusions point
out the moral character of the paternalistic

1Ibid., p. 25.   2Ibid., p. 26.

relationship.[1] The moral element to that relationship is
created by the cultural stress on the values of
reciprocal _amae_.

---

[1]Suzuki, pp. 538-539, Question 5.6., "Type of
Supervisor Preferred:" "Suppose you are working in a
firm. There are two types of department chiefs. Which
of these two would you prefer to work under?
A. A man who always sticks to the work rules and never
demands any unreasonable work, but on the other hand,
never does anything for you personally in matters not
connected with the work.
B. A man who sometimes demands extra work in spite of
rules against it, but on the other hand, looks after you
personally in matters not connected with the work.

	1953	1958	1963	1968
Type A (Non-paternalistic)	12%	14%	13%	12%
Type B (Paternalistic)	85	77	82	84
Other and Don't Know	3	9	5	4

"The fact that 8 out of 10 Japanese adults have
consistently preferred the paternalistic type of supervisor during the fifteen year period measured and that
only slightly more than 1 in 10 have preferred the
non-paternalistic type is evidence of the strong
persistance of this paternalistically-inclined characteristic. The overwhelming preference exists at all
ages and in all categories of population breakdown."

In response to the hypothetical question that
similar responses to such a question might be obtained
in other, "non-paternalistic" cultures as well, the analysts make the following point:

"The paternal type /of supervisor/...represents
an important link in the Japanese social chain of care
and help that starts with the parent-child relationship
and grows through the teacher-pupil stage to the
post-academic career....For a person brought up in the
traditional pattern, the non-paternalistic supervisor
gives little assurance of adequate security. It is
definitely a moral decision for the respondent to break
away from the traditional pattern of security to a new,
rather independent way of life."

Allusion to the moral choice between independence
and security (amae) seems to support the value of the
conceptual dichotomy between autonomy and dependency
discussed above, p. 78-79.

4. Decision-Making Without Confrontation

These leadership skills are put to their greatest
test in the process of bringing the group to a consensus
on an issue of group concern. Because open disagreement would be a sign of disunity which would produce
anxiety in a group, the group   leader's principal
test is to orchestrate a decision-making process which
will lead to a consensus without confrontation. A
primary example of this process is that modeled after
the "village meeting" (yoriai).

> In yoriai decision-making, the subtle pre-
> liminary consultation of nemawashi (literally
> "root-trimming") is a prerequisite. Everyone
> must be consulted informally, everyone must be
> heard, but not in such a way that the hearing of
> different opinions develops into opposition.
> The leader and his assistants "harmonize
> opinion" in advance, using go-betweens to avert
> the confrontation of opposing forces. After a
> consensus of opinion is reached by the iteration
> of compromise and minute adjustments behind the
> scenes, the yoriai meeting is held to allow the
> prearranged consensus policy to be suggested and
> for general public acceptance to be demonstrated.
> The ideal result is the "unopposed recommenda-
> tion" or the "unanimous voice." This legiti-
> mates decision: that everyone concerned agrees,
> that the group as a whole is behind it, that it
> is taken in such a way that process and outcome
> enshrine and embody social harmony. Where these
> procedures are not scrupulously followed, the
> result can only be to deprive the decision of
> legitimacy and to perpetuate conflict.[1]

---

[1]Ibid., p. 132. Here we see that the group is
the source of authority; the value of emotional
dependency is the basis for its legitimacy; and a group
decision is accepted so long as it has been arrived at
in a manner which does damage to neither sensibility.

The importance attached to continual consultation
is evidenced in the workings of the various Diet and
party committees involved in the process of introducing
legislation for consideration by Parliament. When a
bill on the floor of the House is non-controversial, it
is so only because all parties have had a share in
planning its formal presentation in advance, in the
House Management Committee. Government and minority
party members of that committee, in planning the agenda
for a floor session, will have received instructions
from their respective Diet Strategy Committees con-
cerning the proposed bill. When all agree that a bill
is non-controversial, a small amount of time is
designated on the agenda for its consideration, which
becomes little more than a staged formality.

Baerwald reports that most legislation is
approved in this fashion, but points out that if all
parties had not taken part in the planning, if each
party had not been given the opportunity to concede
that the bill was non-controversial, its presentation
on the floor would be seen as an affront, as "undemocratic," and a non-controversial bill would find itself
being heatedly debated.[1] In cases when partisan
disagreement does develop, consultation with all

---

[1]Hans H. Baerwald, Japan's Parliament (London:
Cambridge University Press, 1974), p. 85.

parties is equally essential. Even though accomoda-
tion of an ideological minority position may not be
likely, it is important for dissenters to have the
opportunity to "demonstrate their sincerity." By
making the strength of their commitment to an issue
publicly known, dissenters are showing their reason for
disrupting the group process; and they are seeking
indulgence of their behavior (amaeru) on that basis.

The reciprocal dependency in the group is
revealed in the characteristic of decision-making which
Nakane calls "super-subordination." This amae relationship shows clear parallels to the husband-wife relationship described previously:

> ...the relationship between leader and subordi-
> nate is one of mutual dependence. When a leader
> depends very heavily on his subordinate, the
> latter can readily encroach on the domain of his
> leader. Indeed, a subordinate often de facto
> carries the work of his leader and in such a case
> he can extend his latent power over the entire
> group, while making use of his leader's name.[1]

An important example of such a case is the
government ministry in which a Diet politician,
appointed to a cabinet position for reasons quite unrelated to any expertise in the technical field of the
particular ministry, occupies a formal position of
authority over an elite, professional bureaucracy whose

---

[1]Nakane, p. 68.

members fill every rank right up to his vice minister.
Although everyone might recognize the limited technical
knowledge of their appointed superior, to challenge his
authority would be to undermine the unity of the group
as a whole. Indeed, the bureaucrats depend on the
minister to exercise his leadership in a way that pre-
serves the unity and the status of their group; and the
minister depends upon his subordinates to administer
his area of responsibility with the same professional
attention as before his arrival (and after his
departure).

This mutual dependency between leader and
subordinates has been institutionalized in the bureaucratic policy-making procedure known as ringi-sei. It
is "a system of reverential inquiry about a superior's
intentions,"[1] in which an initiative from a lower
official is circulated around a clearly defined route
to the top of the organization. Along the way, the
proposal may be sent back to its drafter with modifica-
tions. But once the proposal reaches the desk of the
group head, bearing the seals of approval from all
intermediate levels of group members, its approval by
the leader is virtually mandatory.

---

[1]For a full analysis of ringi-sei, with an
assessment of its strengths and weaknesses, see Tsuji,
op. cit. Tsuji finds the use of this system (ringisho)
to be somewhat in decline.

In the first place, to object to a measure in the face of such a mature consensus would represent too great a separation between the leader and his group. In the second place, it would signal, in effect, that the leader was no longer predisposed to depend upon his subordinates to act in his (and the group's) best interests. Because of the implicit reciprocity in amae, this deviation would threaten the subordinate group members' sense of security in their relationship of dependency upon their leader. As a consequence, the unity of the group would be damaged (especially in the case of a group which does not enjoy a mature institutional structure to fall back on), and the group itself as an authoritative body--not only for its members, but for outside groups as well--would suffer loss of esteem.

The operation of ringi-sei provides a good illustration of one last characteristic of Japanese decision-making. Because ringi-sei, like any properly conducted consensus-building process, informs everyone concerned and gives everyone an opportunity to contribute to the proposal, an expectation is created that all members will cooperate in its ultimate implementation.[1] This is an expectation arising not simply from sound management practice; it is an expectation

---

[1] Ibid., p. 457.

enforced by the strongest social sanctions. During the informal consensus-building stages conducted covertly within the group (or in ringisho, at the level of other lower officials), the expression of personal opinion is solicited. After the long process of arriving at the group's unified position has been completed, however, everyone's support is demanded. For a group member to openly express disagreement with a decision already made would represent a break from the group of the most unacceptable sort, with the same consequences for group cohesiveness as in the case above. Unless he should first choose to resign, the result for the individual would very likely be ostracism. The harshness of that response indicates the depth of feeling surrounding the group and suggests the sense of outrage which can be provoked by violation of the unwritten rules of amae.

D. Factionalism

The cultivation of an "us" vs. "them" group identity which leads to a perception of other social and professional contacts as outsiders is a final characteristic of Japanese group behavior to be discussed here. It deserves more thorough examination, because this "in-groupism" manifests itself in an outstanding feature of Japanese politics, factionalism.

The faction has been defined as

the primary unit of reference for individual
members of the Liberal Democratic Party (and the
Socialist Party, etc.). Political influence
and its attached symbols such as party and
government office are distributed through the
factions. Each faction is organized in terms of
a leader with his followers. The leader's
influence is maintained through operation of
multiple factors, such as, financial and political rewards at his disposal, personal loyalty of
followers, and the group orientation of individual Diet members.[1]

Halloran goes so far as to describe the faction in
Japanese politics as a "fundamental motivating force."[2]

There are today three principal factions each in
the Japan Socialist Party (JSP) and the Japan Communist
Party (JCP),[3] and not less than nine in the governing
Liberal Democratic Party (LDP). (The Democratic
Socialist Party (DSP) traces its history back to a
faction which bolted from the Socialist Party in 1960.)
Factionalism is characteristic of virtually all group
endeavor in Japan, as will be illustrated later in

---

[1]Roger W. Benjamin and Kan Ori, "Factionalism in
Japanese Politics," Annual Review (Japan Institute of
International Affairs), 5 (1969/70), 76-91.

[2]Richard Halloran, Japan: Images and Realities
(New York: Alfred A. Knopf, 1969), p. 26.

[3]Because of disciplined organizational structure
under strong leadership, factional divisions within the
JCP have been less visible over the past ten years than
in the JSP. Nevertheless, three streams have been
identified as the "China lobby," the Kremlin-oriented
group, and the "nationalist" group. In fact, factional
divisions exist within each.

student activism. Before considering political party factions (habatsu) in particular, some description of factional behavior in general is warranted.

1. "We" vs. "Them"

Since "we" solidarity is affirmed by competitiveness with "them," behavior directed toward promoting and preserving the in-group and its interests is necessarily complemented by behavior that does damage to the position or interests of rival groups. Competitive behavior, from time to time, finds its expression, unhappily, in destructive excesses. The beating death by members of a Tokyo university club of a junior member who was attempting to withdraw from the club is an example of one kind. The beating to death of a Kakumaru-ha (Revolutionary Marxist Faction) member by rival student radicals of the Chukaku-ha (Core Faction) is an example of the other.[1]

From incidents of this sort, the Japanese seem to have learned the destructive potential of open competition when it has broken loose from the restrictions of their highly regulated society. In this respect, factionalism represents one restraining influence to keep that competitiveness under control. The constructive potential in channeling that energy

[1]Lawrence W. Beer, "Japan Turning the Corner," Asian Survey 11, No. 1 (1971), 74-85.

through factions has been pointed out by Beer: "The capacity for organized task-accomplishment by thousands of tight-knit groups may have contributed more than any other single societal factor to Japan's impressive success in many fields."[1]

Similarities to the concept of "sublimation" may be noted here; the parallel is more striking when libidinal drives are equated with amae. In fact, Doi argues that the social restraints such as exist in the regulated behavior patterns in factions have been developed over time precisely for the purpose of imposing controls upon amaeru, whose uninhibited expression would have destructive impact, as shown in the cases mentioned above.[2] That argument must remain in the realm of speculation. It will be seen however, that factions do indeed provide vital outlets for amaeru while encouraging the expression of amae in furthering organizational goals.

Factionalism is a logical concomitant to the "frame" basis and vertical structure of organizations in Japan. Party factions develop only around a leading personality. When that leader is removed, the faction will inevitably change, if not disintegrate. "The survival or disintegration of factions (habatsu)

---

[1]Ibid., 81.   [2]Doi (1962).

within Japanese political parties depends primarily on
the existence of a suitable successor after the death
of the oyabun."[1] According to Nakane, such a "suitable
successor" must be in a position in the group that
enables him to lead the group without destroying the
relations already existing within it; and, realistically,
he must have a sizeable following already attached to
him personally.[2]

    2. Functional and Dysfunctional Aspects of
        Factionalism

The basis of factions in personality and the
consequent importance of personal loyalty as an
influence on political behavior have been attacked by
many reform-minded critics as incompatible with
"rational" government and with the goal of pursuing
broad national interests. Baerwald rebuts: "Factions
and factionalism contribute their share to making Japanese politics more open and competitive. In the context
of Japan's political party system, factionalism is not
only advantageous, but also eminently rational."[3]

The debate over the advantages and disadvantages,
the functionality and dysfunctionality of factions in
Japanese political parties is a continuing one. In

---

[1]Nakane, p. 46.   [2]Ibid., p. 45.

[3]Baerwald (1974), p. 73.

order to draw conclusions about the relationship of
factionalism to _amae_, it will be helpful to summarize
several of the arguments offered on both sides.

a. Organizational Weaknesses

Nakane finds four principal elements of dysfunctionality in factions in general. First, because of
the exclusiveness of the in-group and its competitiveness with outside groups, cooperation between two groups
is virtually impossible unless they can be brought
together through the leadership of a unifying personality acceptable to both groups. This joining of
factions to form a larger whole was achieved by the
Liberal and Democratic Parties in 1955 under the
leadership of influential business and political
figures.[1]

---

[1]Nathaniel B. Thayer, How the Conservatives Rule
Japan (Princeton: Princeton University Press, 1969);
p. 12-14. The Liberal Democratic Party (LDP) continues
to function as a coalition of factions; and even though
their aims are fundamentally the same, factional rivalry
makes it difficult for them to cooperate.

The positive side to this characteristic is a
potential which goes hand in hand with the capability
described above, in the context of competitiveness, to
transfer loyalty to a more broadly defined group of
greater status in the hierarchy. One important result
is that party unity in the LDP is strictly maintained
in the face of opposition from outside the party.

Beer notes: "With a shift in the parameters of
one's in-group from a smaller to a larger unit, loyalty
becomes focused on the larger in-group to the extent and
so long as relations with "outsiders" dictate. Factions
within a political party and subdivisions within a
business firm, ministry, or news media company may

A second drawback considered by Nakane is the suspicion of factions engendered in outsiders by the conflict of group in-fighting.[1] In the public realm, evidence that group energies are being expended to so great an extent on factional rivalry gives rise to questions about the group's "social responsibility." This query has been registered most appropriately in respect to the JSP,[2] whose preoccupation with internal conflict has not helped the JSP's credibility as a political party capable of exercising the powers of government.

Third, the problems of group maintenance in the emotionally demanding faction preoccupy group members,

---

compete freely among themselves, but unanimous loyal support of the higher unit is normally expected in dealings with "outsiders." /Freedom of Information and the Evidentiary Use of Film in Japan," American Political Science Review, 65, No. 4 (1971), 1133./ Beer goes on to show, in the context of the Hakata Film Decision, how the strength shown by such unanimity facilitates compromise even with the courts.

[1]Nakane, p. 55.

[2]Over the years, the leading opposition party has presented the Japanese electorate not with well-formulated alternatives to government policy on substantial issues, but with ideological harangues from rival factions attempting to legitimize their respective claims to party leadership.

For a full history of the JSP, see Allen B. Cole, George O. Totten, and Cecil H. Uyehara, Socialist Parties in Postwar Japan (New Haven: Yale University Press, 1966).

with the result that the achievement of the group's
goals tends to become a matter of only secondary concern.
This dysfunctional characteristic finds its most
repeated and apparent expression in the priority
assigned to unity and harmony. Until an issue has been
brought to a consensus involving all the factions of a
group, action on that issue is deferred. The conviction
that to reach no decision at all is preferable to
risking open disagreement obviously leads to stalemate
from time to time.[1]

A fourth consequence of factionalism is that
stability is maintained within a larger group only at
the expense of one faction's domination of the others.
Because coalitions do not form on a strictly horizontal
basis, an alliance of unequal partners is the only
form in which a group of more than one faction may
survive. "The existence of equally competing powers is
a most unstable situation in Japan; stability always

---

[1]When one considers that the decision-making
machinery of the Japanese government consists of a multitude of factional coalitions--be they parties,
ministerial groups, or interest groups, the impact of
this handicap is clear. The fragile alliance of
coalitions in the LDP and the alignment of competing
powers in the bureaucracy maintain their authority only
so long as they can function and produce results. The
fact that they have, by and large, avoided the sort of
deadlock which would damage that "instrumental"
authority testifies to the unifying effect of the LDP's
status as leader of the Japanese national "group."

resides in imbalance between powers when one dominates the other."[1] The predominance of one faction is necessary to provide the leadership for a group which would otherwise flounder in antagonism and indecision.[2]

In general, then, the weaknesses of factionalism are seen to lie in instability and inhibitions against cooperation. Cohesiveness and stability are promoted, according to Nakane, by 1) the strength of the institutional frame itself, 2) the formal administrative organization, and 3) the status of the group (for example, in terms of its role of importance in society).[3] In the case of the LDP, the Diet offers very little institutional security or identity as a frame in and of itself; the organization of the LDP as a national party is notoriously weak. Long LDP incumbency, however, has fostered an entrenched bureaucracy; and LDP ties to that

---

[1]Nakane, p. 53.

[2]This necessity for imbalance among competing factions as a prerequisite to stability is well illustrated in the Diet (viewed as the group), whose factions (in this case, parties) have been cooperating for the past twenty years under the leadership of the LDP. The limitation imposed by this characteristic is seen in the repeated failure of minority parties to form an effective coalition in opposition to the majority party; to date, none has been willing to be a "follower." For the same reason, a conservative-dominated coalition between the LDP and, for example, the DSP would represent little or no change from the distribution of power existing today.

[3]Ibid., p. 57-58.

mature organizational structure seem to compensate for their own weakness: "freeing the party from the responsibilities of political leadership and enabling it to indulge in power struggles."[1] This "indulging" relationship in the fashion of <u>amae</u> is seen to exist as well between the LDP as a whole and the individual faction, which, "while lurking behind the party shield, feels released from the responsibility necessarily attached to a ruling party and thus frees itself to seek the most opportune moment to ascend to power."[2]

     b. Analyses and Evaluations of Factionalism--
        Summary

Criticism of factionalism is typically made in terms of democratic values of open competitiveness and equal access to power, seen as guarantors of the public interest. Those are clearly not the values whose maximization is being sought by Japanese politics; the first part of this chapter showed that the values being institutionalized are those which preserve the group as the basis of authority in Japanese life--political and otherwise. Several writers of a different mind have justified factionalism in the political parties as

[1]Hiroshi Itoh, ed., <u>Japanese Politics--An Inside View</u> (Ithaca: Cornell University Press, 1973), p. 15.

[2]<u>Ibid</u>.

a healthy adaptation of enduring political values to the requisites of campaigning, fund-raising, and decision-making in a transplanted parliamentary system.[1]

Totten and Kawakami identify three general areas in which factions have a positive role to play. The factions serve as a basis for recruitment of leaders, provision of mutual aid, and development of policy (or ideological) commitments.[2] Totten and Kawakami find no less than eight specific "functions" of factions in the political party system; but it is important to note that they find a significant potential for

---

[1]Evaluating factionalism in the LDP, Baerwald (pp. 72-73) finds three principal strengths. First, factionalism has been an insurance against oligarchical authoritarianism which might (although unlikely so) result from an otherwise unified conservative party. Second, given the continuing domination of one party, factions allow different segments of the Japanese public to have influence (although not so broad a range as ideally might be hoped for). And third, since it is within party pre-parliamentary negotiations that important decisions are made, factions at that stage provide the airing of alternatives which is vital to successful policy-making. Baerwald's evaluative judgments of factionalism, however, are predicated on the prior existence of government by factions. They do not help to answer the question why such a form of government exists.

[2]Goerge O. Totten and Kawakami Tamio, "The Functions of Factionalism in Japanese Politics," Pacific Affairs 38, No. 2 (1965), 109-122.

dysfunctionality in each case as well.[1]

---

[1]First, factions within the LDP are ladders
along which followers may rise with the fortunes of
their leader to positions of party leadership and political power. Dysfunctionally, this method of recruitment effectively excludes able men bound to non-
ascendant leaders. Closely related, and with the same
drawback, is the role of factional strength in providing a basis for the bargaining process involved in
the selection of party leaders.

Third, factionalism within the "one and a
half party system" provides for leadership changes and,
to a lesser degree, policy shifts which would otherwise
be lacking. This, in turn, creates a flexibility which
is essential to party unity. Dysfunctionally, reliance
on the factions as the sole basis for change may result
in quite meaningless leadership and policy changes,
leading over time to greater inflexibility and a consequent loss of authority among rival parties.

Fifth, the factions provide informal lines of
party communication, dysfunctional in the de-emphasis
of formal party structure and the encouragement of
secretiveness in political affairs. At the same time
as assisting the leadership in disseminating guidelines
and maintaining party unity, these channels of communication operate from the bottom up to provide for the
legitimate (i.e., covert) expression of alternative
opinion and diverse interests. Here, the dysfunction
lies in the fact that the diverse interests that might
be represented by different factions within the LDP
still are confined to a relatively narrow sector of the
public.

Seventh, and perhaps most significant, is the
role of factions in financing the election campaigns of
its members. In the LDP this function is especially
important in respect to the eighth factor, namely, the
necessity to maximize electoral support for two or more
conservative candidates in each of the multi-member
electoral districts in Japanese national elections.
(The complexities of the LDP strategy for determining
and supporting not only the right number but the right
balance of candidates in each district are considerable.
They are remarkably well explained by Baerwald, pp.
54-57.) Although factionalism has generally helped the
LDP's successful campaign strategy, it has often

A look at the functions identified by Totten and Kawakami reveals a list of the same functions performed by political parties in any multi-party system: recruitment, interest articulation, stability in change, mobilization, and allocation of resources.[1]   The difference is that these functions are performed by Japanese factions within a much narrower political sphere than by "mass"

---

interfered.   Party unity and growth of the strength and resources of the party as a whole become impossible.

Last are the roles of the factions in respect to ideological issues.   In the first place, factions within the ruling party may adopt a policy initiative made by a rival party, with the result that a proposal made initially as part of an ideological stand may ultimately be incorporated as a pragmatic policy by the government, when it appears to its advantage to do so.   The dysfunction in this potential for incremental compromise is, ironically, that opposition parties have been permanently relegated to a minority status in the Diet.   In the second place, Totten and Kawakami speak of the ideological commitment afforded by factionalism as a factor which keeps public interest high among activists but which blurs the party's image among the general public.   At this point, they suggest that "a faction's ideological position can attract and satisfy its members psychologically" (p. 121).   Although the importance of ideological considerations has been questioned by most other writers, the psychological dimension is the only factor which Totten and Kawakami offer as a function which might uniquely explain factional behavior rather than simply describe it.

[1]Cf. Anthony King, "Political Parties: Some Skeptical Reflections," Comparative Politics: Notes and Readings, Macridis and Brown, eds. (Homewood, Illinois: Dorsey Press, 1972); pp. 233-251.

Western parties. These functions offer nothing in the
way of explanation for the existence of factionalism
in Japan. Clearly, the system works; and because it
works, it continues to. Within that tautology, which
may be seen as a pitfall of such "functional analysis,"
a description of the system becomes its justification.
Too much analysis of Japanese factionalism has followed
such an argument.[1]

Baerwald addresses more squarely the question of
why factions are found in the LDP. First, the LDP at
its very conception was formed by the conjoining of
already existing conservative alignments, brought
together primarily by their common apprehension over
the appearance in 1955 of a newly unified Socialist
Party. Those same alignments continue to exist.[2]

Second, personal antagonism among LDP leaders
developed along several fronts, notably between those
purged and those not purged during the occupation, and
between those who rose to national office through political careers and those who entered politics as retired
bureaucrats. A final explanation seems to be found in
the distinction between the political styles of "high
posture" confrontation and more accomodative "low
posture."[3]

---

[1]For a critical review of scholarly writings on
the subject of factionalism in Japanese politics, please
see Benjamin and Ori, op. cit.

[2]Baerwald, p. 48.   [3]Ibid., p. 58.

Baerwald goes further than Totten and
Kawakami in explaining why differences exist among the
members of the LDP and in describing the issues on
which those differences have become significant; but
his answers fall within the classification of "historical description." The question of why those differences lead specifically to factionalism remains
unanswered.

C. Financing Factionalism

A final characteristic of factionalism needs to
be considered before the tenacity of factions in Japanese politics can be fully appreicated: that is its
costs. Japanese business leaders in particular, who
have borne the escalating costs of Japanese election
campaigns, have expressed concern over this drawback to
factionalism.[1]

---

[1]Business interest groups such as the influential
Keidanren (Federation of Economic Organizations) recognize that because factions are competing with each
other as much as with rival parties, the amount of money
presently spent in electing a conservative majority to
Parliament is unnecessarily high. A strengthened, unified party structure, some argue, would provide one
funding channel for all LDP candidates, would allow for
greater economy and control of expenditures, and would
eliminate the situation existing now in which a consti-
tuent hoping to keep channels of communication open
feels the pressure to make financial contributions to
both the party and a faction leader with whom he may
have a connection.

Their voices reached a crescendo following the blatant use of big money and direct corporate backing of LDP candidates in the highly contested House of Councillors election in July 1974.[1] The evidence of personal enrichment by use of political funds which led to the resignation in November of Prime Minister Tanaka added fuel to the flames of opposition to the habatsu system. The choice of Miki Takeo as a compromise candidate to succeed Tanaka was encouraged by his record as an outspoken critic of factionalism in his party.[2]

Some cynicism may be found in the selection of Miki as Prime Minister. It is doubtful that many of his supporters favored any concrete moves to disarm political factions. Rather, they recognized that such rhetoric served the practical goal of improving LDP

---

[1]Because of the danger that the LDP majority in the upper house might be lost, campaigning was particularly vigorous. See Hans Baerwald, "The Tanabata House of Councillors Election in Japan," Asian Survey, 14, No. 10 (1974), 900-906. "Tanabata" refers to the festival occurring on July 7, the day of the 1974 election.

[2]On July 12, following the House of Councillors election, Miki had resigned his cabinet post as Deputy Premier in protest over the heavy-handed manner in which the LDP campaign had been conducted. Questionable practices included allocating to given corporations full financial responsibility for the successful conduct of assigned candidates' campaigns. It is probably correct to assume, however, that had the LDP strategy succeeded, Miki's resignation would not have been tendered. As it happened, the government majority was cut to a bare minimum.

electoral performance in subsequent elections--a goal
phrased by Miki as "to eliminate the distorted image of
the party in its relations with business enterprise."[1]

A call for reform of LDP financing practices may
not appear on its surface to be an attack on factionalism; dollar figures show that it is. A report of political revenues filed with the Home Ministry shows that
in the first half of 1974 alone, preparatory to the
"Tanabata" election, $172 million were contributed to
1,373 political fund-raising organizations. As one of
those organs, the LDP collected $49 million. The total
reported by all five political parties was $75.9
million, leaving almost $100 million to be accounted
for by clubs, support groups, labor union organs,
factions, and faction-based "research associations."[2]

Clearly, factions have become indispensable
actors in the electoral politics of Japan; and until
another system can be devised for giving money the
voice in politics which it inevitably seeks and for
providing candidates with the financial support necessary for their election, factionalism will not be

-----

[1] New York Times, December 21, 1974; page 2:1.

[2] The Asahi Shinbun reported that LDP expenditures in support of their 95 candidates totalled over
$90 million--far in excess of the $65,000 per candidate
permitted by law. New York Times, July 8, 1974;
page 1:8.

easily abandoned. Past statements by Prime Ministers (and faction leaders!) Ikeda and Satō declaring their intentions to break up factions cannot be taken at face value; certainly no meaningful steps have been taken in that direction. It is doubtful that they could be. Nevertheless, there is no reason to find cynicism in Miki's own words: "Japanese democracy will collapse if the election of Members of Parliament and local assemblies continues to cost too much."[1]

3. The Tenacity of Factions

Why, in the face of expressed disenchantment among the business community, criticism of alleged dysfunctionality, and building concern over the future of democratic politics in Japan, does factionalism persist with such tenacity? Totten and Kawakami have alluded to the psychological gains from ideological commitment which might account for the

---

[1]New York Times, December 22, 1974, iv, p. 2.

personal motivation behind factionalism.[1] Nakamura,
however, argues that the sharing of beliefs is
secondary to the emphasis on the limited human nexus--
even within religious sects.[2]

For the parties of the left, policy differences
appear to be a continuing rationale for factionalism;
yet the distinct possibility exists that conflict over
ideological issues is being used to perpetuate factional
groupings which are valued for entirely different
reasons.[3] Within the LDP, doctrinal differences

---

[1]Supra., p. 113, n. 2 (cont'd).

[2]Nakamura, pp. 481-482.

In Japan there exists a strong tendency
toward sectarianism and factionalism, which is
another manifestation of the tendency to regard
as absolute any limited and specific human nexus.
It is a fact generally observed today that this
tendency to clannishness is still prevalent in
Japan even though it is not a phenomenon of recent
origin, but has its deep roots in ancient Japanese history.

I should like to dwell upon this tendency
first in reference to the constitutional make-up
of the Buddhist order and the mode of worship
among the believers. In Japanese Buddhism, for
the most part, it is not the universal creed that
is counted most important. But rather, the
emphasis has been placed upon the specific religious order itself as a limited and concrete
human nexus.

[3]On this score Baerwald expresses bemused puzzle-
ment: "One is never certain whether advocacy of an
alternative policy contributes to factional strife, or,
conversely, that the requirements of factionalism demand
the espousal of substitute ideas." Baerwald, Japan's
Parliament, p. 58.

generally play a minimal role; factional membership is
based almost entirely around personal relationships and
the support which accrues within those relationships.[1]

The nature of that support, of course, is twofold:
financial and psychological. Financial backing could
be acquired through other channels; the needed emotional
support cannot. Herein lies the explanatory power of
amae: amae is the motivation shared by most Japanese
that leads them to seek the "limited human nexus,"
whether in political factions or other primary groups
in Japanese society.

E. The Explanatory Power of Amae

Amae offers more than a description, more than a
model, more than a paradigm of factional behavior: it
explains that behavior in terms of human needs. The
explanatory power of amae goes beyond

> those works which deal with Japanese factionalism
> in terms of different sorts of causal explana-
> tions /in terms of which t/he cultural patterns
> of oyabun-kobun relationships, obligations and

---

[1]Initially, considerations of general policy
preference will influence the decision of the candidate
with a choice among alternative factions. Generally,
however, policy issues are of secondary importance only
within each faction. This is shown by the fact that
the right wing Sierankai group has been formed in the
LDP strictly on the basis of common orientation on
foreign policy issues, yet without causing the disruption of its members' primary factional ties.

> loyalty, and familial behavior patterns are
> cited as providing deep seated models for inter-
> action that predispose the Japanese to a factional
> style of politics.[1]

The shortcoming of such studies lies not in the

invalidity of those patterns, but in the fact that they,

too, are as much effects as causes. Chapter 2 examined

patterns of family relations not only to illustrate

prototypical amae relationships, but to document the

learning process which makes amae significant to adult

behavior. In Chapter 3 I explained on-giri and the

manifest values of loyalty and obligation not just as a

paradigm for social relations, but as a formal and

sanctioned expression of the internalized values of

amae. And in the first part of this chapter, the oya-ko

pattern and the complex vertical structure built upon

it have been treated not only as organizational goals,

but as vital characteristics of Japanese society that

have been shaped to fulfill the fundamental emotional

needs of amae.[2] Befu makes that connection clearly:

---

[1]Benjamin and Ori, 78.

[2]For an organization using human energies, it is
obviously advantageous for the fulfillment of human
needs to be adopted as an organizational goal as well;
and the exploitative potential in claims of successfully
equating the two has been given due attention elsewhere.
It need only be said here that amae is a dependency need
far more subtle, and, hopefully, more intrinsically
human, than anything in the power of either feudal or
fascist rulers to distort.

"The close interpersonal ties that develop between the superior and his subordinates...do so because of the need to prevail upon others for affect."[1]

Factionalism, then, represents one of the most visible institutions in Japanese politics which exists not only to serve a variety of functions common to most political systems--and in a manner consistent with the cultural values and social mores of Japan, but also to provide needed channels for the self-expression in amaeru. It is in this respect that factionalism represents a political institutionalization of amae: a "structural set of role patterns" which fulfills the individual emotional needs of amae and encourages their expression in socially constructive ways. In turn, the socio-psychological forces toward group conformism are legitimized by the unwritten rules supporting reciprocal amae.

The causality of amae is supported by the "deviant case approach" advocated by Benjamin and Ori. If factionalism were to be abolished, the place of factions would have to be taken by some other form of organization. Nakane sees only two alternative forms: one built on "contract" relationships, the other built

---

[1]Befu (1975), 151.

on horizontal relationships. Her conclusion confirms the emotional basis of factionalism in the personality structure of the Japanese: "such a system would not find favor with the Japanese without some fundamental change in the Japanese character."[1]

Chapter 6 will assess the possibilities for such change, including attitudes toward "contract" and horizontal relationships. First, however, I will report on two examples of institutionalized _amae_ which appear not only in organizational structure, but in ritualized political behavior. It is suggested that factionalism, student radicalism, and the "permanent opposition" in Japan are only three major patterns of political behavior among many others which may be far better understood as having a unique basis in the _amae_ culture of Japan.

---

[1]Nakane, p. 79.

CHAPTER V

AMAE AND THE POLITICS OF OPPOSITION

A highly visible authority system to depend
upon is at the same time a highly visible target to
revolt against. Revolt in Japan of the sort which
would reconstitute society along new lines of authority
or which would express a radically different consensus
on basic values of living is not in the offing for
Japan. It is in the nature of the Japanese process of
consensus building that such an abrupt change in
widely held views could occur only under near anomic
conditions. The strong Japanese embrace of
"democurashi" after defeat in war offers an example of
that possibility. But even a turnabout of such
seemingly revolutionary impact as that was made possible
only by the continued operation of the much stronger
political value of an implicit trust and dependency
upon those in authority, for whom at that time the
word "democracy" was a vital key to open the doors to
power in the new post-war order.

Quite apart from revolutionary challenge to Japanese political values, however, there occur regular
examples of rebellion from very much within the

socio-political mainstream of Japan.[1] Most political demonstrations, as well as the official response to them, are ritualistic in nature. One is tempted to inquire whether these expressions of conflict may be viewed more accurately as arising from within the more traditional attitudes toward authority described in previous chapters or from within the newer spirit of participatory democracy. The answer, certainly, is that both are important.

The source of political protest to be considered first is the organizations of politically active university students. From the radical-democratic ideological content of the student movements, it might well be argued that their activities take small impetus from Japan's post-war identity as a constitutional democracy. Whether this or the opposite may be the case, this section is concerned with showing how student radicalism today manifests the more deeply-ingrained patterns of amae.

The second major group in opposition to the leadership and policies of the Japanese government is

---

[1]This distinction between revolution and rebellion follows the analysis made by Max Gluckman, Politics, Law and Ritual in Tribal Society (Oxford: Basil Blackwell, 1965). For further discussion of this point, see infra., p. 135.

the broad alliance of minority political parties and organized labor organizations. Their protest activities, in turn, will also be examined in the light of their amae relationship to the government party and to society at large.

A. The Student in Japanese Society

Among nations with traditions of Confucianist ethics and administration by an educationally-defined elite, the intellectual community is a particularly reasonable locus for political activism. The May 4th Movement (1919) in Republican China and the March 1 Movement (1919) in colonial Korea are prime historical examples of Asian revolutionary movements led by intellectuals and composed principally of student activists.[1]

Although the bakufu government (c. 1600-1867) in Japan placed a premium on martial skills for entry into the elite warrior class (bushi), the development of body and spirit were not to be undertaken apart from the development of the mind. And although less

---

[1]On the subject of these historic movements see, respectively, Chow tse Tung, The May 4th Movement (Cambridge: Harvard University Press, 1960), and K. Lee, "The March First Movement," Listening to Korea: A Korean Anthology, comp. Marshall R. Pihl (New York: Praeger Publishing Co., 1973).

Confucianist in tradition than her mainland neighbors,
Japan has developed since the Meiji Restoration a
recruitment system for its governmental and managerial
elite which relies   every bit as heavily as its
imperial Chinese counterpart on academic examination.[1]
Smith comments:

> The Meiji state shifted Japan to the ideal of an
> examination-selected elite, but the basic vision
> of a natural elite remained. The students of
> Tokyo Imperial University in the twentieth cen-
> tury would of course be reluctant to admit a
> "Confucian" content to their image of their own
> role in society, for this orientation was
> largely western. Yet beneath the western
> rhetoric, they were very much the heirs of the
> Tokugawa samurai. This consciousness, unarticu-
> lated as it may have been, gave the imperial
> universities a high potential for student
> radicalism.

The "examination hell" of the Japanese student
reaches its culmination in the college entrance examinations given every Spring. At that critical juncture,
performance determines, for all intents and purposes,
how high in the bureaucratic, corporate, or academic
elites the candidate may climb. But for years before

---

[1]From 1869 to 1945 a system of civil service
examinations modeled after the Prussian bureaucracy
gave the appearance of an impartial meritocracy. Nevertheless, graduates of the Law Faculty of Tokyo Imperial
University provided the majority of high level bureaucrats. Robert M. Spaulding, Jr., Imperial Japan's
Higher Civil Service Examinations (Princeton: Princeton
University Press, 1967).

[2]Henry DeWitt Smith, II, Japan's First Student
Radicals (Cambridge: Harvard University Press, 1972),
p. 8.

then, myri   lesser examinations lead the student from
one level   education to another--and into
institutions of varying degrees of excellence and
preparatory promise.

A system of school cliques includes lineages
that begin with the founding of universities in the
late nineteenth century under the increasing influence
of western educational approaches. This system of
gakubatsu (school factions), combined with the tutorial
approach to university education, and reinforced by
the paternalistic elements in the student-teacher relationship, means that once admission to a prestigious
university has been won through examination, a student's
place in the leadership echelons of society is very
nearly assured, should he choose it.[1]

With this understanding of the position of the
university student in Japanese society, it is clear
that his rebellion represents opposition very much from
the inside of the social system, rather than from
outside and "over against" it. By viewing that position
in relation to both the student's past--parentally-
directed striving for academic achievement, and his
future--a choice among fairly well delineated and

------

[1]The importance of academic background to the
career pattern of a bureaucrat is shown in Kubota Akira,
Higher Civil Servants in Post-War Japan (Princeton:
Princeton University Press, 1969).

limited career alternatives,[1] the significance of _amae_
to his activities as a university student is forcefully
suggested.

B. The Role of _Amae_ in Student Activities

The operation of _amae_ may be seen in three
general instances in the relationship between student
radicals on the one hand and society as a whole and its
authority figures in particular on the other.

1. Permissiveness in a Society of Controls

University life is clearly the last opportunity
for juvenile self-indulgence before an adult assumes
the responsibilities of earning a living and supporting
a family. Japanese society is not unique in this
respect. It is unique, however, in the stringency of
codes of behavior which surround the manner in which
the Japanese adult must properly conduct his professional and family affairs. Accordingly, the dramatic
change between student radicalism and professional
moderation in the life of a Japanese university graduate
has become famous as "employment conversion"
(shūshoku tenkō).[2]

---

[1]Note that these are alternatives which, once
chosen, are secure for the individual and protected by
the system of social values as a whole.

[2]This pattern of changes at graduation has recently been challenged in a study by Ellis S. Krauss, Japanese Radicals Revisited (Berkeley: University of California Press, 1974).

The significance of amae to student radicalism
may be seen in the first instance, then, as the student's
own perception of himself in the last role which he may
play until old age in which not only his immediate
family but society as a whole will be indulgent of his
excesses. As Beer points out, this permissive tendency
among adults is reinforced in Japan by the value placed
on spiritual strength and single-mindedness (makoto),
even as it manifests itself in potentially destructive,
and indeed, self-destructive actions.[1]

Smith draws a connection between early modern
permissiveness of student disruption and a carry-over
from the traditional military emphasis in education
until the end of Tokugawa Japan:[2]

> Even after the military emphasis in higher
> education disappeared in early Meiji, bellicosity
> survived. Both education and society as a whole
> exhibited a high degree of tolerance for student
> rowdiness, perhaps less from awe of students
> than in the age-old conviction that boys will be
> boys.

2. Student Group Formation

In the second instance, amae is a strong motivation for student radicalism in much the same way as we
have seen it operating in ordinary adult activities,
namely, through the group.

---

[1]Beer, in lecture at University of Colorado, 1974.
[2]Smith, p. 21.

Very commonly, a successful student will maintain close ties to his faculty advisor, known to the
student always as sensei (teacher, or more literally,
he who has gone before one in life). Ideally, the
primacy of this relationship will be maintained
throughout life, as illustrated by the often-recounted
story of Tokyo Governor Minobe's much acclaimed, but
nevertheless equally called for and anticipated visit
to his sensei before deciding whether or not to run
for that public office.[1] Because this relationship
incorporates all the elements of the oya-ko pattern,
it is a close personal bond as well, embodying the
human feelings implicit in the reciprocity of
giri-ninjo.

None of this contradicts the fact that, at
appropriate times, students will dedicate themselves
with utmost intensity to the radical activities of a
student political group--be it the dominant faction of

---

[1]Nakane, p. 43.

the campus Zengakuren[1] or a more ad hoc group. This
represents an upward transference of loyalty from
primary ties to groups formed under professors; and it
is facilitated precisely by the fact that the
teachings and ideological persuasions of some faculty
members at leading universities offer direct encouragement and support for the radical students' goals, if
not for their more violent methods.

The activist group, then, does not represent a
competing focus of loyalty and amae, but includes and
enlarges upon the group of peers defined first by the
student's primary academic ties. This fact has been
cited more than once to explain the obvious reluctance

---

[1]Zengakuren, the All-Japan Federation of Student
Self-Governing Associations, far from being a unified
student movement, is a term often used to embrace a
broad spectrum of student organizations whose ideological
orientations are mutually repugnant. Because student
self-governing associations on a majority of campuses
have been dominated recently by factions sympathetic to
the Japan Communist Party (JCP), factions to the left
reject the label or qualify it by hyphenation, such as
Zengakuren-Sampa. For present purposes it need only be
borne in mind that the recent history of student radicalism is an ongoing struggle for ideological legitimacy and
tactical predominance among not less than fourteen factions of Marxist, Trotskyist, Maoist, and other colora-
tions. Supporters of the JCP and its student organization, Minsei, constitute a majority, but they are considered by the "New Left" and its descendants to be
moderate and collaborationist. For a full but somewhat
dated exposition of factional lineages and doctrinal
differences, see Sunada Ichiro, "The Thought and Behavior
of Zengakuren: Trends in the Japanese Student Movement."
Asian Survey, 9, No. 6 (1969), 457-474.

of faculty members to denounce or discipline student
demonstrators whose excesses were well within the
spirit of their own radical teachings.[1]

Among the exceptional, ultra-radical student
groups whose excesses come to light from time to time,
group conformism is enforced with such force and sometimes brutality that there would appear to be no room
left for even _amaeru_ in the group concerned. The most
spectacular example of recent note was the bloody purge
in 1972 by the notorious Red Army Faction of fourteen
of its members deemed to be "too soft."[2] Although
ideological conformance is of concern within radical
factions, pathological examples of that sort are rare.[3]

Greater freedom exists in most student groups,
and conflict arises more commonly over antagonisms
between competing factions than within the same group.
Nevertheless, as DeVos shows, the emotional dynamics
within the group are a powerful motivation affecting
normal student radical behavior:[4]

---

[1]See, for example, DeVos, p. 424; and Lawrence
W. Beer, "Japan 1969: 'My Homeism' and Political
Struggle." _Asian Survey_, 10, No. 1 (1970), 44.

[2]DeVos, p. 432.

[3]For other examples, see Beer (1971), pp. 75-76,
and _supra_., p. 103.

[4]_Ibid_., p. 436.

> It is estimated that at the present time two
> thirds of the total of one and a half million
> university students belong to some form of stu-
> dent self-government association. The faction
> of the Zengakuren that controls a university or
> a department also controls the revenues from
> membership fees, and this operates as a kind of
> 'closed shop' in which students have no alterna-
> tive but to join the faction in control....
> At the beginning of every school term the stu-
> dents not only pay their fees for tuition, but
> they are almost required, by sanctioning of the
> student body itself, also to pay assessments to
> the particular organization that has control.
> Thus a politically organized sanctioning body is
> in control, and the students, whether they are
> politically interested or not, are coerced by
> group atmosphere to join in the activities.

Public awareness of this factor in student

demonstrations has probably contributed to society's

willingness to put up with the disruptions which have

become ritual in university communities. And it is in

the spirit of amae that authority figures wait out the

childishness, in the full confidence that order will be

restored and that in return for their indulgence, com-

pliance with that order will be won. Rather than force

their will on dissident students by use of arms,

police take only such measures as may be well-advised

to insure that no undue damage to life or property is

suffered in the course of the tantrum. Particularly

entertaining was the example of Tokyo authorities

going to considerable pain and expense to remove from

the streets all loose paving stones which might other-

wise be used destructively in a protest march to be

permitted along that route.[1]

The ritualistic nature of student "demo," seen
not only in their customary decorum, but in the group
exuberance and other characteristics which liken them
to Japanese religious festivals, shows that amae serves
a very profound function in keeping order. It is significant not simply in the strong social control
exercised by consensus on the value of amae, but as it
relates to a pressure-release function in society which
has been considered by Max Gluckman in his study of
tribal African social systems.[2]

For Gluckman, conflict is inherent in society;
and rituals may be used in a given society to provide
legitimate expression to those conflicts. Where those
rituals are based around existing social relations, as
student demonstrations in Japan clearly are, they serve
to reaffirm the social order and individuals' roles in
it. "In short, the prescribed statement of social conflict affirms that there is a solidarity--and that when
you ritually act (note, 'act', not 'act out') your
institutional hostility, it is to strengthen the moral
values implicit in the system."[3] In Japan, existing

---

[1]Ibid.

[2]Gluckman, op. cit.

[3]Ibid., p. 259.

sensitivity to amae permits and even facilitates this institutional expression of conflict.[1] In return, the effect of these legitimate challenges is to affirm the social solidarity of amae and to strengthen the moral values expressed in amae.

3. Confrontation and Manipulation

n containing civil disturbances of very large size, and confronting them only when necessary, specialized riot forces equip themselves protectively with helmets, masks, shields, and armored vehicles. They arm themselves only with clubs, with the salutary consequence of only three civilian deaths from riot action against demonstrations over the past twenty-five years.[2] Despite this impressive restraint on the part of authorities, students have attempted to portray themselves as aggrieved parties and to develop sympathy for themselves among the population as a whole. In this third

---

[1]As a result, it encourages the expression of new ideas and accomodates change at a manageable rate. This is in contrast to less open societies, such as contemporary South Korea, where student protest is systematically repressed. I have discussed the destructive potential in this denial of a ritual acting of conflict in a paper, "The Value of Freedom of Expression in South Korea," presented at the Western Conference, Association for Asian Studies, October 1975.

[2]The deaths were not caused by police, who abandoned the use of firearms in 1952. For comprehensive study of Japanese law enforcement, see David H. Bayley, Forces of Order (Berkeley: University of California Press, 1976).

context, considerations of amae help to explain the recent increase in violent, confrontational tactics used by student demonstrators in terms of the anticipated gain in popular support produced by "victim consciousness."

In order to distinguish between the more spontaneous and idealistic activism of the early 1960's and the well-orchestrated and more cynical radicalism since then, let us consider briefly the highlights of student demo's in recent Japan.

a. From Passive Resistance to Active Confrontation

The zenith in the activism of the student radical movement in Japan must be seen as the University Crisis of 1968-1969,[1] which effectively closed down the leading academic institutions of Japan for a prolonged period of time. But the activism of that time differs in considerable measure from the activism of the earlier 1960's. The U.S.-Japan Security Treaty Crisis of 1960 has been described as the greatest mass movement in Japan's political history.[2] But because of the central role played in that "Ampo" struggle by political actors

---

[1]See Beer (1970), 43-45.

[2]Robert A. Scalapino and Junnosuke Masumi, Parties and Politics in Contemporary Japan (Berkeley: University of California Press, 1962), p. 125.

other than students, it will be described in more
detail below. Nevertheless, the evolution of new confrontational tactics over the decade between these two
major upheavals shows a significant change in the role
of amae in radical behavior and in popular response to
it.

During the latter half of the 1960's, in the
continuing spirit of the milestone Ampo Struggle of
1960, student activism against U.S. involvement and
Japanese complicity in Viet Nam took the form of non-
violent mass demonstrations. Such demonstrations of
passive resistance, often coordinated by Beiheiren
anti-war activists, drew considerable moral support,
but had no impact on official policy.

Beginning in 1967, however, and due to the
increasing influence of a small number of radical activists from outside the dominant factions of established
Zengakuren chapters, direct and often violent con-
frontations between demonstrators and police became
the rule rather than the exception. Two incidents at
Haneda Airport signaled the new tactics, as students
blockaded the airport, physically resisted police
efforts to remove them, and even tried to lie in the
path of taxiing aircraft in their attempt to prevent
Prime Minister Satō from making trips to Saigon and

Washington.[1] Incidents during 1968 included prominently
the opposition to the opening of a U.S. Army field
hospital in Oji, attempts to stop the servicing in
Shinjuku of trains transporting U.S. jet fuel, an
assault against the Headquarters of the Self-Defense
Forces, and the escalated level of opposition to
land-clearing efforts in preparation for construction
of an international airport in Narita.[2] All these
skirmishes, in addition to the staging by over 5,000
students of simultaneous outbreaks throughout Tokyo on
International Anti-War Day gave substance to the term
"street battle" used to describe the incidents.

> b. The University Crisis of 1968-1969

This pattern of increasingly irresponsible
activity was finally introduced onto university campuses, where existing student self-government associations (mostly dominated by moderate leftists
affiliated with the JCP) were pre-empted by more
radical, "anti-Yoyogi" (i.e., anti-Communist)
activists.

After the formation of an All Campus Joint
Struggle Committee (Zenkyōtō), leaders would characteristically direct the occupation and barricading of

---

[1]Sunada, 466.   [2]Ibid., 468.

campus buildings, and the university administrators
would be presented with a list of non-negotiable
demands. In mass bargaining sessions that would ensue,
faculty would often be insulted and sometimes subjected
to a kangaroo court.[1] Sporadically throughout the
Zenkyōtō insurrection on campus, violent skirmishes
would take place between the controlling faction and
rival factions, usually characterized by the anti-
Yoyogi leaders as communist obstructionists and
subverters.

In most cases, and particularly after the
passage in August 1969 of the University Law,[2] police
forces were brought onto campuses to overcome and eject
the radical minority. This final act in the play of
student violence was to be the most important for the
radicals. Sunada expresses the mentality with which
some radical leaders approached these new,

---

[1]Several suicides among faculty members resulted
at different institutions, apparently related to sub-
jection to this indignity.

[2]The University Temporary Management Measures
Law was enacted in the face of persisting support for
the notion of university sanctuary, in order to return
order to the country's immobilized university system.
By placing full responsibility for the continued functioning of each campus on its administrators--and by
providing for the interruption of pay to faculty at
campuses which were not functioning, the law encouraged
administrators to request police assistance on dis-
rupted campuses. Beer (1970), 44.

confrontational tactics, or <u>jitsuryoku soshi</u>
("prevent by using force"):[1]

> So-called "confrontation tactics" are usually
> employed by radicals in order to expose the
> brutal aspects of the power structure so as to
> 'politicize' or further radicalize mass
> bystanders. If by promoting violent clashes
> they seem intentionally to seek brutal suppres-
> sion by the police, it is because they are
> generally much more concerned with the political
> effect their tactics will bring than with vic-
> tory in the immediate confrontation.

The "political effect" being striven for is what Doi

refers to as <u>higaisha ishiki</u>, a sense of victimization.[1]

More specifically, what the students hope to produce is

a widespread popular identification with the students

as victims, or in other words, a mass "victim

consciousness."

    c. <u>Amae</u> and Victim Consciousness

In understanding the <u>amae</u> content in victim

consciousness, the importance of guilt once again comes

to the fore.

In his study of the survivors of the Hiroshima

nuclear explosion (<u>hibakusha</u>), Robert Lifton makes

clear that their external deformations are minor wounds

in comparison with the psychological scars of guilt

which most carry still, because they survived what

countless others did not. Lifton concludes that the

---

[1]Sunada, 466.   [2]Doi (1973), p. 26.

sense of victimization that hibakusha feel comes
primarily not from the handicaps or ostracism they
suffer, but from their persisting burden of "guilt over
survival priority."[1]

Because of the privileges which one enjoys, as
in the case of Lifton's interviewees, whose privilege
was in their having lived through the holocaust, guilt
arises. In the case of activist university students,
whose privileged place in society is undeniable, guilt
induces them to try to achieve a sense of fellow-feeling
with those perceived as victimized by that society. A
prime example is the vigorous student involvement in
support of local farmers' efforts to resist relocation
from the site of the proposed Narita airport.[2]

Because this identification with such victims
is, psychoanalytically, in the form of activist
self-denial, the student becomes a casualty of his own
guilt, and a victim himself. Doi interprets student
violence accordingly: "In this sense they become
victims themselves and begin to abuse those who ignore
the victims or, more positively, attack those

---

[1]Robert Jap Lifton, Death in Life (New York:
Random House, 1967), p. 7. Lifton notes that in
referring to hibakusha, the term higaisha is more
commonly used.

[2]For an excellent account of the"Narita Incident," see Roger Wilson Bowen, "The Narita Conflict."
Asian Survey, 15, No. 7 (1975), 598-615.

responsible. The more unnatural the denial of self
that provides the starting point, the more bellicose
and violence-prone will be the action that stems from
it."[1]

The involvement of outsiders in this sense of
victimization arises in a related manner; as Doi
expresses it, "this kind of sense of victimization can
be seen as harboring a doubly convoluted amae
mentality."[2] Just as students identify with certain
"victims," so they hope to have a wider public identify
with them as the victims which they have purposefully
become. As will be seen from the example that follows,
this identification on the part of a larger segment of
society is possible especially because the sense of
being victimized derives from unsatisfied amae.

In the minds of student leaders, victim consciousness was to be formed on the basis of the popular perception that student groups, acting in pure single-minded
pursuit of youthful ideals had been brutally suppressed
by an insincere and undemocratic government. As a
victim, as Gibney defines the term, the student radical
would be perceived as "a person whose sense of amae has

---

[1]Doi (1973), p. 162. [2]Ibid.

been betrayed and abused."[1] Student radicals, in other
words, hoped to win the sympathy of the people by
appealing to their usual benevolence toward student
self-indulgence and then to win the support of those
people against the authorities who, by not tolerating
them, would be seen as having violated the unwritten
social contract of amae.

   4. The Boundaries of Violent Opposition

   That strategy of the 1969 Joint Struggle Committees failed, as indicated by popular polls taken during
and soon after that time. Although police were called
onto campuses to restore order in over 300 instances
in the course of 1969,[2] and in spite of a record of
over 8000 students arrested (and one third of them
indicted) in the time between the Haneda Airport incidents and late November 1969,[3] student activists
suffered a loss of support among the general public.

   In a poll taken in the wake of the university
crisis, cited by Beer and DeVos, 75% of the respondents

---

[1]Gibney, p. 127. Gibney points out that this
same sensitivity to amae leads citizens groups who are
presenting grievances to characterize themselves not as
"protest" groups, but as "victim" groups. As will be
seen in the discussion of citizens movements in Chapter
6, this characterization is particularly fitting for
anti-pollution demonstrators.

[2]Beer (1970), 44.   [3]Sunada, 473.

approved of protest meetings, and a majority recognized that students and university administrators both shared responsibility for the conflict. Quite apart from a wide acceptance of student goals (reinforced by admiration for youthful sincerity), however, was a clear rejection of the students' choice of methods. DeVos reports that 81% regarded striking or non-attendance as inappropriate, and 92% were opposed to the occupation of buildings and the use of picket lines.[1] If there has been, as DeVos characterizes it, "a wave of public revulsion against immoderate idealism,"[2] it has grown out of an almost universal disenchantment with the increased resort to violence. (Among all age groups polled, none registered higher than 2% in support of student violence.)[3]

Public outrage over student violence seems to have reached its height following the murder of three policemen at the most vicious stage in the five-year-long (1967-1971) course of hostilities known collectively as the Narita Incident, mentioned above. The advocates of jitsuryoku soshi, by openly announcing their intentions to demonstrate in advance of each incident,[4] had shown their disapproval of "guerrilla-type" or terrorist

---

[1]DeVos, p. 433.   [2]Ibid., p. 424.

[3]Beer (1970), 46.   [4]Sunada, 467.

actions. By contrast, the student leaders involved in
the Narita conflict (imitating, apparently, the tactics
of the Viet Cong, in whose war they saw themselves as
joining) introduced in late 1967 the tactics of
guerrilla warfare, particularly in their use of raids
and attrition.[1] The battle between expropriating
authorities and the fortified resisters escalated
through thousands of injuries and hundreds of arrests
until September 17, 1971, when three policemen were
found clubbed and burned to death. Bowen summarizes
well the general reaction of the public:[2]

> "Stop! You have gone too far. You have
> exceeded that level of violence which our society
> is willing to tolerate."
> This reaction, the notion that the students
> had gone too far, had within it an implicit
> belief that there are, in fact, limits to accept-
> able violence. Although the Japanese public had
> become accustomed to a great deal of violence
> during the postwar years, mainly arising from
> student and labor demonstrations, they were
> accustomed only to violence at a "controlled"
> level, and to violence carried out in a
> more-or-less routinized fashion. That policmen
> and students would sustain minor injuries during
> "struggles" was expected and even tolerable:
> "This kind of minor violence has always taken
> place, and probably always will. I guess it
> just goes with being a student. And besides,
> hardly anyone ever gets hurt very badly." But
> murder, and premeditated at that (several
> factions had announced their intent to kill
> policemen), was intolerable; this brutal act
> fell outside the "rules" of protest tacitly
> accepted by most Japanese.

---

[1]Bowen, 599.   [2]Ibid., 614-615.

The fact that the resistance on the Narita site virtually disappeared from the day following the news of the murders indicates an awareness among most students as well of what the bounds of acceptable social protest are.[1]

5. Conclusion

That the use of violent confrontational tactics should have created a backlash aimed squarely at the group of radical leaders who introduced it testifies to the basic sensitivity of the Japanese public to the fact that <u>Zenkyoto</u> radicals were not conducting the ritual of student activism "according to the rules."[2] Thus, as millions of TV viewers across Japan watched the live drama of the "battle of Todai" on January 18 and 19, 1969, they must have been struck not by the victimization of the student belligerents, but by their excesses. They must have noted that their spray of

---

[1] It should be pointed out that terrorist actions such as the 1972 bombing at Lod Airport in Tel Aviv and the 1975 mass kidnapping in Kuala Lumpur, conducted by members of the underground Red Army Faction, are aberrations which are universally condemned by activists in the universities.

[2] The behavior of the students in the radical groups themselves during the university crisis gives further evidence that the "rules of the game," especially as inferred from Nakane's conclusions about group formation, were not being observed. That is, participants moved casually from one faction to another, as well as in and out of the movement itself. Beer (1970), 47.

molotov cocktails was met only with the spray of water
hoses, and that their shower of rocks and glass from
high atop the Tokyo University auditorium building was
not sufficient to deter the methodical advance of the
police, once they finally determined that the students
had been given ample time to "demonstrate their
sincerity." They might also have remarked the final,
and perhaps overly-generous act of indulgence as the
victorious police permitted the die-hard student legions
to join in a last refrain of the "Internationale" before
being removed from the beseiged building. Thus subdued,
the students did not resist arrest, but were curiously
passive.

What was clearly in evidence was that the
restraint of the authorities was in keeping throughout
with the rules of amae and that the excesses of the
students went beyond them. On that basis, the leaders
could not have hoped to arouse a sense of their victimization, since neither the authorities nor the general
public had any reason to feel guilt for the treatment
of the students. This, in a sense, is the greatest
success of the unique Japanese riot control forces.

The interplay of increasingly self-conscious
students with methodically restrained police and with
a remarkably tolerant populace gives further insights
into the ubiquity of amae in Japanese politics.

Consider the words of Narushima Ryuhoku,
spoken at the opening ceremonies in 1882 of what is
now Waseda University: "I expect to see from the Tokyo
Senmon Gakko the emergence not of these clever types
who give in to authority and seek only their own security,
but rather of virtuous men who will ever seek to devote
themselves truly to the people."[1]

If by his words (as underscored) we understand
one political (or more correctly, apolitical) aspect of
amaeru, it is ironical that students to this day have
expressed their rebellion against that ethic in a
manner which is totally in keeping with it. And the
causes in which they see themselves devoted to the
people are pursued with a zeal which must surely be
indebted to a tacit understanding of their relationship
to government and society as a whole in terms of the
unifying bonds of amae.

Another element of amae in political protest has
been shown unwittingly by Rollo May, whose insight con-
sequently suggests the cross-cultural significance of
that Japanese term: "Protest is half-developed will.
Dependent, like the child on parents, it borrows its
impetus from its enemy."[2]

---

[1]Smith cites Ozaki Shiro, Waseda Daigaku (1953);
p. 14.

[2]Rollo May, Love and Will (New York: W. W. Norton and Co., Inc., 1969), p. 193.

C. Partisan Politics and Problems of Loyal Opposition

An unmistakable parallel to students' rebellion in Japan is the similar outbursts of childlike protestation occasionally indulged in by their elders among the representatives of the people in the National Diet. This section will show how the politicians who are members of the minority parties in the legislature incorporate the values of amae strongly into their roles as seemingly perpetual members of an institutionalized political opposition.

A fundamental question posed in the operation of virtually all forms of government in contemporary Asia, but especially important, of course, for representative governments like Japan, is whether or not a viable expression of "loyal opposition" can be accepted as legitimate not only by those in power, but by the population concerned as well.

It is not unreasonable to assume that political opposition in China today is regarded much in the same way as in imperial times, namely, that if it demonstrated its power by succeeding to power, it was authoritative, but if it failed, it was exposed as illegitimate. In pre-modern China, a ruling dynasty was said to possess imperial power because it enjoyed the "mandate of heaven." Whenever one dynasty were overthrown, it was at once a result and a sign of the fact that the defeated Emperor had fallen from grace. The cycle was, of course, repeated. In that way, the "mandate of heaven" neatly defined away the problem of a "loyal opposition" in China.

In Korea, a critical characteristic of authoritative rule has been unanimity among the decision-makers. That political dissent is regarded only as a "luxury" is revealed by the government's intolerance for political opposition in South Korea today.[1] Hahm Pyong Choon has shown how former attitudes persist today in the fact that a Korean judge registers his dissent from the majority opinion in a ruling at the risk not only of discrediting the decision, but of undermining the legitimacy of the court as a body.[2]

The Japanese experience with political parties and their open competitiveness for support distinguishes Japan from both China and Korea.[3] The place of the opposition is fully incorporated into Japan's political system; however, it is not incorporated as an equal to the parliamentary majority. An evaluation of the

---

[1]See paper by Mitchell, op. cit.

[2]Hahm Pyong Choon, "The Decision Process in Korea," Schubert and Danelski, eds., Comparative Judicial Behavior (New York: Oxford University Press, 1967).

[3]See Robert A. Scalapino, Democracy and the Party Movement in Prewar Japan (Berkeley: University of California Press, 1953).

minority parties in the light of _amae_ will give
insight into their status in Japanese politics, and
will help explain the behavior of the "loyal" opposition in Japan.

    1.   The Liberal Democratic Party and Control of
          the Parliamentary Process

    In understanding the behavior of the minority
parties in the National Diet, it is necessary to see
how well-entrenched is the majority and how completely
it controls the parliamentary process, as but one part
of the machine of government.

    In November 1955, largely in response to the
challenge of a reunified socialist camp, leaders of
Japan's two conservative parties were brought together
to constitute one dominant party, the Liberal-Democratic
Party. Although the LDP's share of the popular vote in
parliamentary elections has declined to less than 40%
in the last national election in 1974,[1] they have
capitalized on long-standing incumbency and have been
able to use to best advantage the disproportionately
rural districting scheme of multi-member single vote
districts.[2] Without interruption since its formation,

---

[1]This percentage represents the performance of upper house candidates running in local (prefectural) districts and does not include the showing of LDP candidates
for the nation-wide constituencies. Baerwald, "The Tanabata House of Councillors Election in Japan," 900.

[2]The Public Office Election Law, under which the
number of Diet seats are allocated to each district, was
found to have been unconstitutional at the time of the
1972 national elections by an April 1976 holding of the
Supreme Court. Japan Times, April 15, 1976, p. 1.

the LDP has remained the government party in close
relationship with the bureaucracy whose retired members
help fill its candidacy rosters and with the business
community to whose interests the party's fortunes are
tied.

This strong collaboration between the government
party and bureaucracy has been institutionalized in the
daily operation of the Japanese parliamentary government. Accordingly, the opportunity for input into the
decision-making process by members of the opposition
has become largely ritualized, with the result that
the greatest power wielded by the minority is in the
negative form of obstructing the legislative process.

To give a better understanding of the limits of
opposition in Japanese government, the following
description outlines briefly the law-making process and
shows how it effectively minimizes the role of the
minority parties in the Diet.

Almost all legislation of importance is initiated
and drafted by the government bureaucracy, characteristically through the group process described in Chapter 4.[1]

---

[1] A further extra-legislative ordinance power is
every bit as significant as the bureaucracy's legislative initiative; and since this second policy-making
process, encountered most widely as "administrative
guidance," by-passes the Diet and public scrutiny entirely, it removes the opposition even further from the
governmental function. For a description of "administrative guidance" in its various forms and a discussion of
its authority in light of Article 41 of the Constitution,
see Yamanouchi (1974), 22-33.

Working in close contact with the professionals in the
ministries and other executive agencies is the LDP
Political Affairs Research Council. Although the nature
of this relationship remains partially hidden, Chalmers
Johnson suggests that most direction is provided by the
bureaucrats, since the Political Affairs Research
Council is recognized to be the exclusive preserve of
former bureaucrats within the LDP.[1]

The most challenging task in the process of
passing legislation appears to be arriving at an agreement among the ministries themselves, who are typically
protective of their own "territory" and functional
jurisdictions. After that agreement has been achieved,
the process of guiding the draft legislation through
party councils, cabinet bureaus, and finally Diet
committees is often pro forma. Since it is only at the
last stage that the political opposition has an opportunity to have input to this process, it is no wonder
that their criticism receives little attention from
LDP Dietmen.

LDP members, of course, are bound by strict party
discipline to vote as a bloc in support of government
measures, both in committee and on the floor of the two

---

[1]Johnson (1975), 8-9.

houses. Because committee membership in the lower house is assigned in proportion to the numerical strength of each party in the house, the LDP is assured of prevailing in committee ballotting as well as in plenary session of the house. In the House of Representatives, every standing committee chairman is an LDP member, further assuring that committee deliberations are favorable to government proposals.[1]

The hegemony of the LDP is further reinforced by the relationship between legislative committee, ministry, and party council. Of sixteen standing committees in each house, twelve have jurisdiction in areas paralleling those of government ministries. A close working relationship exists between legislature and ministry in which committee research staffs are composed largely of senior bureaucrats from the corresponding ministry.[2] In addition, there is a direct link between Diet committees and the LDP's principal policy-making body, the Policy Affairs Research Council. The Council consists of a division for each ministry, which results in a correspondence as well to Diet committees. The conservative members of the standing committees in both houses sit as members of their corresponding divisions within

---

[1]Baerwald, Japan's Parliament, p. 94.

[2]Ibid., p. 101.

the Policy Affairs Research Council.[1]

These facts clearly indicate that once consensus has been affirmed in the LDP party organ and the government initiative has been confirmed as party policy, a position has been reached which will allow no deviation or public compromise, such as might be called for by members of the opposition in a committee hearing. So it is apparent that once LDP Executive Council approval has been given to proposals forwarded from the bureaucracy by the Policy Affairs Research Council, and after the Cabinet Legislative Bureau finalizes the draft legislation, and the LDP Policy Committee and the Diet Steering Committee determine the strategy for guiding the bill through to passage, partisan action has little meaningful role to play, especially not openly.

In some cases, a positive legislative contribution can be made by members of a minority party in committee. The situation may arise in which a minority member has presented a counter-proposal to a government bill. In fact, many government bills are responses to popular proposals made by the opposition. Misawa shows that by virtue of the LDP's control of the parliamentary process, such an opposition-formulated measure may be effectively pigeon-holed until the government bill,

---

[1]Thayer, p. 210.

incorporating the desirable features of the original,
is produced.[1] Thus, publicity generated by committee
hearings is reserved for the government-sponsored
legislation, and all opposition measures, even those
predating the majority proposals, are handled as
counter-proposals. Such pre-emption may even include
plagiarism of certain portions of the opposition bill.

The best that the opposition can hope for is
that LDP leaders will direct the committee chairman to
present a bill or an amendment as a joint proposal
(usually done with bills serving vested interests).
However, "no single bill proposed by opposition parties
presented as a counter-proposal to an LDP bill has
received the Diet's approval."[2]

Over the years, especially since the consolidation of the conservative bloc into one party, party
positions on all sides, determined in advance of the
parliamentary debate, have reduced that debate to
nothing more than government publicity and partisan
attack, with increasingly little opportunity for compromise or negotiation. For the most part, therefore,
the legislative resources of the opposition are not
positive actions of a partisan equal, but manipulative

[1]Misawa Shigeo, "An Outline of the Policy-Making
Process in Japan," Japanese Politics: An Inside View,
ed. Hiroshi Itoh (Ithaca: Cornell University Press,
1973), p. 34.

[2]Ibid.

actions of a dependent participant in government.

2. *Amae* and the Permanent Opposition

The continuing majority status of the LDP must,
however, be credited in part to the minority parties
themselves, whose behavior over the years has done much
to condemn them to perennial opposition status.

The first characteristic of the opposition to be
noted briefly is its typical preoccupation with dogma
at the expense of attention to substantive issues more
meaningful for the voting public. Ideological questions
in the issues surrounding the role of the Emperor, the
Constitution, foreign policy alternatives and the
Self-Defense Forces have dominated for many years the
political debate among the opposition, with much of the
criticism directed inward against their own numbers.
The JCP has only recently taken heed of this criticism
and given ideological purity less emphasis than the
business of getting its candidates elected. The
"lovable" image, however, and methodical tactics of
identifying with citizens' causes at local levels still
have a great deal of popular antipathy to communism to
overcome.

This widespread suspicion of the parties of the
left is a second characteristic. It springs primarily
from the perception of them as parties whose allegiance
is owed to an entity other than Japan. That such an
allegiance were owed to an ideology would be cause

enough; but many see a disloyal or traitorous potential
in doctrinal ties to the leadership of communist-bloc
countries. This attitude dates back to the nationalistic
reaction to post-World War I Comintern internationalism.[1]
Stockwin claims that JSP extremism and foreign policy
dogmatism have had relatively little impact on the JSP's
electoral position, which is primarily dependent upon
the resources and support of Sōhyō.[2] But until turning
toward "livelihood" issues and hopping on the "kogai"
("environmental hazard") bandwagon in 1969-70, the
largest opposition party in Japan was gaining few new
supporters.

The ideological preoccupation and the divisive-
ness which it feeds are both consequences in great

---

[1]A representative expression of this reaction is
found in Kodama Yoshio, I Was Defeated (Tokyo: Radiopress, 1959), p. 13.

> My aversion to the labor movement lay in the
> fact that in addition to the avowed purpose of the
> labor unions to fight against the capitalistic ex-
> ploitation of labor, it was commonly known that
> the leaders of the labor unions were secretly
> seeking to spread communism and bring about the
> realization of communist ideals. In other words,
> I felt that the communists were working systemati-
> cally to gain the support of workers as a pre-
> requisite to the launching of their Marxist revo-
> lution. It was difficult for me to understand why
> the Soviet Union should have to be called our
> motherland and why Marxism should be forced upon
> a Japan differing fundamentally in conditions from
> Russia, in order just to solve the labor-capital
> dispute."

[2]J.A.A. Stockwin, The Japanese Socialist Party and
Neutralism (Carlton, Victoria: Melbourne University
Press, 1968), p. 157.

measure of a third characteristic, factionalism. To a
greater degree than has been true for the LDP, factional
divisions have imposed significant limitations on the
electoral performance of the principal minority parties.
So also has animosity among the different parties of the
left inhibited their development into a coalition which
might offer a viable challenge to the LDP majority.[1]

I suggest that there is another perception of
these parties held by a significant number of Japanese;
and the opposition parties may be posed with their
greatest challenge in overcoming it. This is the view
of them as children in the political arena who must be
indulged, who must be allowed to amaeru.

A paradox lies in the fact that by effectively
denying direct power to the opposition parties, the
majority legitimizes their use of manipulative,
amae-derived power. The LDP's domination of the
parliamentary process creates in the first place the
concrete situation in which the opposition has little
recourse but to behave unharmoniously when it strongly
dissents from government policy. But precisely
because of the opposition's resulting status as junior
members in the Diet, the majority is obliged not only

---

[1]See discussion of the dysfunctions of factionalism, supra., pp. 105-110.

to consider benevolently the requests of members of
the same in-group (to the degree that the Diet as a
whole constitutes such an in-group), but to indulge as
well the childish outbursts of members whose only
remaining means of exercising control is by amaeru.
This is a paradox which seems inherent in the incorpora-
tion of reciprocal amae in the democratic process of
parliamentary politics, dominated as it must be by one
party.[1]

The amae nature of the opposition's relationship
to the majority is best seen in the confrontational
and obstructionist tactics used by the minority parties,
illustrated most dramatically in the Security Treaty
Crisis of 1960 and the Japan-Korea Peace Treaty Crisis
of 1965. These incidents assumed crisis proportion
largely because the Japanese electorate recognized the
tacit amae relationship between the government party
and the opposition. The opposition was able to enlist
wide popular support and even to bring into question the
authority of the government leaders by arguing, in
effect, that the majority was not performing its duties
in that relationship. The opposition, in other words,
was not being allowed to amaeru sufficiently.

---

[1]Supra., p. 108.

3. 1960 U.S.-Japan Security Treaty Crisis

The major political issue of 1960 was the
ratification of a revised security treaty which had
been negotiated between the United States and Japan.
The new treaty, as had been the case with the original
treaty of 1951, was the object of considerable opposition in Japan, arising for a variety of reasons. As an
extension of a treaty "imposed" during American occupation, the security pact was seen by some as a continuing
limitation upon Japan's independence.[1] Some national-
ists loathed the Japanese position of military
dependency upon the United States. Pacifists feared
the holocaust in which the Japanese people might be
the unwitting victims of nuclear exchange between their
United States ally and the Soviet Union. Neutralists
echoing that fear advocated the end of alignment with
the United States. Some did so more cynically than
others, hoping to encourage a swing away from
"imperialist" ties and to generate greater sympathy for
the Soviet position. The revision of the treaty was
an issue which had been brewing for several years
prior to 1960; but it was in 1960 in particular, after

---

[1]The revised treaty was, in fact, considerably
more equitable in its terms than the original.

the negotiated pact was submitted for ratification, that the many voices of opposition clamored to be heard.[1]

The revised treaty was introduced into the House of Representatives on February 4, 1960, and the Special Committee on the Security Treaty was established with LDP Dietman Ozawa Saeki as chairman. Following its policy of opposition to the treaty, the Japan Socialist Party employed all the parliamentary tactics available to them to delay consideration of the treaty and the related bills whose passage was necessary to effect its provisions. These tactics range from proposing amendments and presenting petitions to creating disorder in committee rooms and employing the "cow walk" method of ballot-casting, which interminably prolongs a vote on the house floor. By keeping discussion focused on two or three clauses and obstructing the progress of the treaty through the channels of ratification, the JSP hoped to block ratification during the regular Diet session. Short of that political victory, delay would at least insure a prolonged debate over the measure, in which the JSP

---

[1]The following narration is based primarily on the reporting by George R. Packard, Protest in Tokyo (Princeton: Princeton University Press, 1966), and by Robert Scalapino and Junnosuke Masumi, op. cit.

would have the fullest opportunity to attack the government and score what points they could in presenting their opposition to the public.

The government, increasingly identified during this crisis with the beleagured Prime Minister, Kishi Nobusuke, wanted not to be forced into the politically disadvantageous move of extending the Diet session. And as the longest debate in Diet history dragged on unproductively, and with no prospect for JSP agreement to an extension (in exchange, for example, for compromise on another point), the Liberal Democratic Party leadership adopted May 19 as its deadline for approval, so that a ratified treaty could be presented, in effect, as a diplomatic gift of welcome to President Eisenhower on the occasion of his planned visit a month later.[1]

Kishi's growing unpopularity gave added impetus to non-support of his government's keystone legislation; and the U-2 incident on May 2 created an atmosphere of international tension which gave greater credence to the socialists' claim of U.S. exploitation and aggression. In addition, it directly touched the Japanese nerves so sensitive to the dimmest prospect of nuclear war. Opposition which was originally quite perfunctory and left for the most part to the JSP

_____

[1]A treaty ratified in the lower house of the Diet becomes law 30 days thereafter if not approved before that time by the House of Councillors.

politicians and their supporters in Sōhyō gradually
attracted wider participation by the press, students,
and the established intelligentsia. The treaty
became a primary issue in the Spring offensive conducted annually by organized labor; and the intensity
of student demonstrations and non-violent sit-ins
increased.

JSP obstruction inside the Diet went beyond the
usual parliamentary techniques and delaying tactics
to include fist-fights and blockading of LDP leaders'
seats, causing such unceremonious scenes as Dietmen
with members on their shoulders charging an opposition
cordon. After 100 days of acrimony and no sign of
progress toward an agreement on the treaty--and in
fact, with increasing prospects of abandonment by
several LDP factions, the mainstream factions undertook
a series of swift and efficient maneuvers to outflank
the opposition.

The "May 19 incident" is described in detail
elsewhere,[1] but a summary here serves to point out
those actions which were to be denounced by the opposition as "undemocratic" and which made the May 19
incident a cause celebre outside the Diet as well as
within.

---

[1]See especially Packard, pp. 237-242.

On the morning of May 18, the LDP submitted its
proposal for a fifty day extension of the Diet session.
The needed Steering Committee approval was won only
after a shoving match led JSP and DSP members to walk
out of the "improper" meeting. On the basis of approval
of the measure by the LDP committeemen thus left to
themselves, a plenary session of the House was called.
JSP members and strongmen described as "secretaries"
blocked the House Speaker in his office by staging a
mass sit-down in the Diet hallway. While skirmishes
were fought between LDP and JSP members inside the Diet,
15,000 demonstrators led by Sōhyō union supporters
confronted 5000 policemen outside the Diet. Two
thousand police were later brought inside the Diet compound at the request of LDP leaders.

> At this point, in the first surprise move of the
> day, Chairman Ozawa called for the Special Com-
> mittee on the Treaty to reconvene, with members
> of all parties present. Nishimura Rikiya and
> Matsumoto Shichirō (both JSP) stood and presented
> non-confidence motions to the Chairman, and at
> the same time, Shiikuma Saburō (LDP) proposed
> that the debate be ended and a vote taken. For
> the next two minutes there was so much confusion
> that the Diet proceedings do not record the
> events. The Socialists, shouting and harassing
> the Chairman, walked out of the room as Ozawa
> announced closure, took the vote, and declared
> that the treaty and related bills were approved.[1]

---

[1] Ibid., p. 240.

After warning the JSP blockaders, Speaker Kiyose
called in 500 policemen, in a move with only one
precedent in history, to enter the Diet chambers and
physically remove (literally, "uproot") the Socialist
Dietmen from the floor. The Speaker was able to call
the plenary session to order shortly before midnight.
Because other opposition members elected to absent themselves from the session, LDP members unanimously
approved a Diet extension. Then fifteen minutes after
closing the session of May 18, that of May 19 was con-
vened. The treaty was reported favorably from the
Special Committee and approved by a vote of the House
in which "all present rose."

This unilateral action to terminate debate and
bring the treaty to a ratifying vote was in response not
only to exasperating opposition obstructionism, but also
to the increasingly precarious majority of the current
mainstream factions within the LDP itself, who were
suffering from growing dissatisfaction with Prime
Minister Kishi. Kishi was recognized not to be predisposed toward compromise with the opposition, and was
characterized by the term "high-posture," denoting
inflexibility.[1] Because of his background as a pre-war

---

[1]Hans Baerwald, "An Aspect of Japanese Parliamentary Politics," Japan Interpreter, 6, No. 2 (1970),
p. 196.

bureaucrat, his "railroad" tactics were denounced as the insolence typical of the pre-war bureaucracy; and because of his unpopularity, Kishi became the symbolic target for the outcry against the outrages of May 19.

As a result of that outcry, which mobilized millions of Japanese and led to violent confrontation, injury, and even the death of a co-ed in a police battle inside the Diet compound,[1] Japan was faced with its greatest political crisis since 1945.[2] Soon after ratification occurred automatically on June 19, and the visit of President Eisenhower had been called off, the crisis subsided. But Kishi's powers of leadership were spent; he announced his resignation on June 23.

D. Amae and the Meaning of Japanese Democracy

Clearly, there was cause for outrage following the events culminating on May 19; but why did the expression of that disenchantment assume such crisis proportions? And clearly, Prime Minister Kishi's position within the LDP at the time was not secure;

---

[1]Although violent exchanges between police and demonstrators warranted the characterization "battle," the student was not killed by direct police action, but by being trampled under foot by fellow demonstrators.

[2]In the largest demonstration of its kind, a "non-political" general strike on June 4 involved a number of union workers and sympathizers estimated by some to be as high as 5.6 million. Packard, 258.

(it was, in fact, partly because of that precariousness that he particularly wanted the new treaty as a feather in his cap). But why did the treaty incident make Kishi the object of such vitriolic abuse? The answer to these questions lies in the fact that the actions of the government in the May 19 incident were widely perceived not as normal recourse in ending legislative impasse, but as a violation of a value which is a source of political and constitutional legitimacy in Japan--violation of the "social contract" of amae. Because of the strong feelings attached to that value, its contravention evoked a widespread emotional response.

Although I can point to no statements to the effect that the government had erred in not allowing the opposition to amaeru, that consideration was a significant part of the 1960 Security Treaty crisis. Because amae is in many respects not consciously operating in the Japanese mind, and seldom articulated in the contexts with which we have been dealing, its expression must be identified in the course of what has already been explained as the political operation of amae. News comments and public criticism of the events of May 1960 give good insights into the sensitivity to amae which underlay the sense of injury to Japanese democracy.

Remarks by the chief editorial writer for the Asahi Shinbun reveal the belief shared by many that government intransigence was much more to be deplored than the equally inflexible obstructionism of the opposition.[1]

> If only...Prime Minister Kishi had shown a little more honesty and sincerity toward the nation in dealing with the question, and if only he had shed his tough, autocratic skin to reveal just a little more humanity, the split between left and right in the nation would almost certainly have been much less severe.

In Japan as in most countries the party in power is a more satisfying target of criticism, and the press assists in directing attention toward the errors of the incumbents. But in Japan, the expectation, rooted in amae, that the government party in its position of authority must indulge the excesses of the minority adds to the strength of sympathy for the opposition when strains in the relationship appear. That the responsibilities of the successful leader should be described in terms of honesty, sincerity, and humanity confirms our picture of an authority figure who obtains compliance (i.e., willingness to work out a consensus on the issues) in return for indulgence and the emotional reassurance in human feelingness.

------

[1]Packard, p. 243. Quoted from Ryū Shintarō, "What Happened in Japan? A Symposium," Japan Quarterly 7, No. 4 (1960), 413.

As has been pointd out, Kishi's low tolerance level for give and take with the opposition was already a point of criticism. But he and other LDP members, it might well be argued, could hardly be blamed for feeling that over one hundred days had been sufficient time for the opposition to make their point and then to demonstrate their willingness to restore order. The response sought by amaeru, on other words, had been made.

The position of the opposition on this point, however, was expressed in a Mainichi Shinbun editorial.[1]

> In view of the fact that doubts about the new treaty continue to exist despite more than 100 days of deliberations...we had repeatedly called for thorough deliberations through extension of the session and for dissolution of the lower house thereafter to ascertain the public's opinion.

Although these goals may have been unrealistic, they were consistent with the opposition view that the government had been dictatorial in arriving at the terms of the treaty and was from the beginning unwilling to participate "sincerely" in a discussion of the treaty and its terms. That predictable JSP dogmatism would have characterized such discussion was certainly a consideration in the government's position, and one with which many of the Japanese electorate would sympathize.

---

[1]Ibid., p. 246. Quoted from Mainichi Shinbun, May 20, 1960.

Nevertheless, accusations of "tyranny of the majority" struck a theme with which opposition sympathizers were able to win the support of many Japanese.

> It is because deliberations and debate are held only superficially and attempts are made to decide the issue from the beginning on the strength of numbers that the strange phrase which is peculiar to Japan, "violence of the majority" is used.[1]

The popular revulsion at such "undemocratic procedure"-- defined not in terms of Diet rules broken, but in terms of the government's insensitivity, or lack of humanity, in regard to the minority's position--reveals a great deal about the meaning of "democracy" in Japan. _Amae_ is central to that meaning.

---

[1]Ibid., p. 247. Quoted from _Asashi Shinbun_, May 21, 1960.

CHAPTER VI

LAW AND THE VALUES OF AMAE

I have shown that amae is fundamental to the
sense of legitimacy in government among Japanese. This
"moral" basis of legitimacy, of course, must co-exist
with the legal basis established statutorily under the
constitution. It is the particular mixture of informal
and formal controls which gives the Japanese group its
unique influence in the lives of individuals; likewise,
it is the equivalent mixture of written and unwritten
laws which gives Japanese law its characteristic flavor.

Many of the operative characteristics of amae
which I have described so far fall well within the
realm of law, in this "informal" sense. The unwritten
rules of on-giri, the "in-groups" determination of what
is and what is not "loyal" behavior, and the arbitrary
definition of the point at which a subject presenting
a petition in Tokugawa Japan no longer warrants indulgence, but punishment instead, are all examples--either
in the past, present, or both--of clear restraints on
political and social behavior which find no formal
expression, but which are enforced by sanctions of the
most extreme sort.

> The unwritten rules of society, rather than for-
> mal law or political power, seem to define the
> limits of freedom in Japan. In behavioral terms,
> in-group constraints on individual freedom seem
> to weigh much more heavily than governmental
> restraints in the balance which Japanese strike
> between freedom and social discipline....[1]

These restraints, which might appear to be anathema to

the rule of law established under democratic constitu-

tionalism, remain in force as customary or "living" law

because of a continuing consensus on the values which

they uphold. Primary among those values is the

reciprocity of amae.

In this chapter I will illustrate how amae

interacts with legalism to shape the administration of

justice in Japan. The nature of the "contract" rela-

tionship will be reviewed in the light of amae, with

particular attention to the concept of "rights." The

recent political phenomenon of citizens' movements

(shimin undō) and government response to it will be

analyzed as a point of convergence for amae and

rights-consciousness. Finally, evidence of change in

the balance between the two will be assessed.

---

[1]Lawrence W. Beer, "Freedom of Information and
The Evidentiary Use of Film in Japan: Law and Socio-
politics in East Asia," American Political Science
Review, 65, No. 4 (1971), 1122.

A. Amae and Extra-legal Restraint

The influence of groupism as a factor in
extra-legal social control is a well-acknowledged
characteristic of the legal environment in Japan.[1]
That characteristic may be viewed as a positive and
stabilizing force within society or as a negative,
inhibiting force on the full realization of individual
freedom.

Group belongingness mitigates legalism in support of the group member's secure status in his society.
As an illustration, Nakane describes a situation in
which formal charges are brought against an individual.[2]
The nurturant group continues to support him: his
relationship with other group members does not suffer;
and his livelihood is not threatened. But the immediacy
of the group and its informal power allow its judgments
--arrived at without the benefit of any "due process"--
to be potentially far more damaging than those of the
formal judicial structure. "An accusation serious
enough to lead to loss of career may well arise out of
a man's unhappy personal relations with his fellows."[3]

---

[1]For example, David H. Bayley, "The Future of
Social Control in Japan."

[2]Nakane, p. 122.   [3]Ibid.

The extent of the extra-legal sanctioning power
of the group is illustrated by the unusual example
reported by von Mehren.[1]   Malfeasance on the part of
some village officials in conjunction with local
elections was brought to the attention of the public
procurators' office by the daughter of a policeman in
the village. The leaders were arrested; and the
village responded by ostracizing the policeman's entire
family.[2] Gradually the group pressure eroded the
procurators' praise for the girl's courage and even the
support of the government's Civil Liberties Bureau.
The incident finally included the forced resignation of
the girl's teacher, who "should have taught the girl
better manners."

> The power and influence of the group not only
> affects and enters into the individual's actions;
> it alters even his ideas and ways of thinking.
> Individual autonomy is minimized. When this
> happens, the point where group or public life
> ends and where private life begins no longer can
> be distinguished. There are those who perceive
> this as a danger, an encroachment on their
> dignity as individuals; on the other hand, others

---

[1] Arthur Taylor von Mehren, ed., Law in Japan:
The Legal Order in a Changing Society (Cambridge: Harvard University Press, 1963), p. 426.

[2] The Japanese expression for village ostracism
reflects the severity of that action. Mura hachibu, or
"eights part village" signifies that out of ten aspects
to life, the community is the basis for eight.
Ostracism, then, effectively cuts its victim off from
those eight parts of life.

feel safer in total group consciousness. There seems little doubt that the latter group is in the majority.[1]

The conflict between these two tendencies-- toward security in the group and toward autonomy as an individual--may be presented most forcefully to the person formally accused of wrong-doing. If an individual were brought to trial to face criminal charges, he would be most likely to plead guilty, and make a display of his repentance. Within the _amae_ ethic of Japan, this behavior results not in loss of face but in the quickest and most easily accomplished re-acceptance by and re-entry into his group. This is because a guilty plea is not taken to be an admission of wrong-doing, but of disrupting social harmony--willfully or otherwise. It is seen instead as a sincere move to restore that harmony. Even as recently as the post-war years, an individual who may have felt himself to have been especially aggrieved was better advised to plead guilty with mitigating circumstances than to press for his vindication as an individual and risk the judge's unsympathetic reaction to such an unrepentant stance.[2]

Patently, the operation of _amae_ in Japanese society poses problems for the exercise of individual freedom, as it has been understood in western societies.

---

[1]Nakane, p. 10.   [2]von Mehren, p. 429.

Freedom (<u>jiyū</u>) as it has been valued in Japanese
society, in fact, may be most clearly understood not as
the free exercise of rights (<u>kenri</u>, a term in existence
only for the last century), but as the freedom to
<u>amaeru</u>.[1] Because <u>amaeru</u> demands a dependent relation-
ship with others by whom one may be indulged in the
expression of this freedom, it is a freedom whose exercise is inherently limited by others--as well as
invited by them.

In Japan as in the United States, the weight of
the law is thrown behind the protection of individual
freedom; but in Japan it supports also the distinctive
freedom to <u>amaeru</u>. Because it is the group setting in
which that freedom can best be exercised, the rules of
group behavior which maintain cohesion--even at the
expense of other "freedoms"--are legitimized by <u>amae</u>.

1. Conciliation as a Group Priority and Legal
Value

The <u>oyabun-kobun</u> relationship in the group
structure particularly creates an informal channel for
adjudication in Japanese communities that derives its
authority from the values of group process.

---

[1]Doi (1973), p. 84.

Traditionally, "reconcilement" was an extra-judicial means of settling a dispute between two people in a patriarchical relationship.[1] Even though a decision reached by reconcilement may not have satisfied the subordinate member, and may in fact have been imposed on him, the decision was accepted because of the expectation that the superior would fulfill the moral obligations of the oya-ko relationship by exercising his power for the best interests of his subordinate.

More significant, "conciliation" introduces a senior go-between in a dispute between two others in order to create, in effect, two interlocking oya-ko relationships in which reconcilement can take place. In other words, a mediator who offers his good offices or, less frequently, an arbitrator who renders a decision is creating a vertical link and building a quasi-group within which the two disputants must reach or be brought to an agreement.

Dan Henderson's study has documented the primacy of conciliation in Japan as the means to bring disputes to resolution, not only in Tokugawa times but today.[2] This approach to adjudication reflects not only the

---

[1]Kawashima Takeyoshi, "Dispute Resolution in Contemporary Japan," Law in Japan, von Mehren, ed., p. 50.

[2]Dan Fenno Henderson, Conciliation and Japanese Law (2 vols.) (Seattle: University of Washington Press, 1965).

Confucian values which stress the restitution of harmony and de-emphasize assignment of right or wrong in a dispute; it reflects as well the unique Japanese value of _amae_. The authoritativeness of "reconcilement" springs from the expectation that the reciprocity of _amae_ will be upheld; the creation of the tri-partite group in conciliation opens the channels through which those same legitimizing values can be mobilized in support of the agreement and the process by which it was reached, much in the manner of decision-making described in Chapter IV. As will be seen in the following discussion, this emphasis on conciliation leads to a formulation of legal rights not as "justiciable rights," but as "conciliable rights."[1]

2. Contracts in Japan

In any legal system, informal means to resolve a dispute short of litigation may be found; and Japanese have a well-documented aversion to litigation. But Japan is unique in the degree to which litigiousness can be avoided not only by recourse to extra-legal means, but by the adjudicative approach within the formal legal system as well. In civil law, this characteristic is owed largely to the Japanese resistance to the western concept of "contract" and the reliance, instead, on the unwritten "contract" of _amae_.

----

[1] Beer (1968), p. 213.

a. The _Amae_ Relationship

The notion of contract in this country and other
western nations creates an expectation among the parties
that various provisions of the contract will be met.
The notion of _amae_ in Japan also creates such an expectation. It is in this respect that I have loosely used
the terms "contract" and "social contract" in relation
to _amae_. Differences between the two notions of contract outweigh similarities, however.

In the first place, the contract in the west
creates a "right" on the part of each party to demand
performance from the other. Because of the universalis-
tic nature of the contract relationship in the west,
failure to perform results in default on the contract;
the defaulted party recovers what value he can from the
relationship; and then it is ended. In Japan, on the
other hand, the contract has the force not only of legal
institutions, but of moral consensus. Ideally, the
establishment of a contract relationship in Japan
involves prolonged discussion and mandatory amenities
so that by the time a formal, contractual tie has been
successfully negotiated, an informal, "functionally
diffuse" and personal tie exists as well.

As should be clearly understood by now, the importance of the latter tie is held to be far greater than

that of the former, but even the former tie is
characterized by amae:

> Japanese do not have a sufficiently clear con-
> ception of such legal terms but honor and trust
> jojo (the surrounding circumstances), giri
> (moral or social obligations to others), ninjō
> (human feeling), yujō (friendship), magokoro
> (sincerity) and so forth...It is perhaps
> well-known that Americans observe contractual
> obligations more closely than Japanese. Con-
> versely, an American will say that he is not
> responsible for what he did not agree to. When
> a Japanese makes an agreement with another
> person, the good will and friendship that gave
> rise to the agreement is more important to him
> than the agreement itself.[1]

The relationship operates in the following general way:
A and B enter into a contract when they feel secure in
their mutual dependency. The contract, to them,
expresses the goals which each hopes to achieve in the
relationship. Because it is a personal relationship
which will not be terminated simply by the conclusion
of one commercial transaction, those goals can be
viewed in a fairly long-term perspective if necessary.
Even though A's performance by a specified time might
be wished by B, A's failure to perform by that time
would hopefully not be a cause for litigation. Because
of the trust which ideally exists in this relationship,
B would not accuse A of wrong-doing, but would instead
be understanding of the difficulties which must have

---

[1]Kawashima Takeyoshi, "The Legal Consciousness
of Contract in Japan," Law in Japan: An Annual, Vol. 7
(1974), pp. 6-7.

led to A's inability to perform. A, of course, who
has committed himself to B in a very personal way,
expects not to be insulted by B's introduction of cold
and impersonal litigation into their relationship.
Rather, if he should not be able to meet the goals of
the contract, he expects to be indulged by B within
their amae relationship. Written contracts typically
contain indefinite provisions, which are sources of
flexibility and security, and "confer in good faith" or
"harmonious settlement" clauses, establishing that "if
a problem arises, it is understood that predetermined
rights and duties will not be asserted, that the
parties will consult (hanashiai o suru) and settle the
matter."[1] This expectation, as we have found in discussing giri-ninjo, carries with it considerable moral
force which in a very real way is stronger than the
legal force which might be brought to perform. This
fact is a very important consideration not only in
Japanese domestic transactions, but in relations with
foreign countries as well.

Legal action in Japan has shown that this moral
force is recognized and is incorporated into the dicta
of court decisions dealing with problems in contract
law. Kawashima cites a 1929 decision as an early
illustration of this characteristic. The court was

---

[1] Ibid., p. 4.

called upon to determine the extent of a contractual
obligation to indemnify an employee, which was expressed
as an unlimited and absolute obligation. The Korean
High Court concluded that the terms should be interpreted as "provisions for indemnity within appropriate
limits."[1] Those limits were to be determined by consideration of such factors as the health of the business
the financial condition of the employee at the time of
entering into the contract, and the relationship
between the employee and the indemnifying surety. This
decision was incorporated into the Personal Suretyship
Law of 1933.

A second area where contract relationships might
be expected especially to lend themselves to the
influence of amae is the field of bidding for government
contracts, or a private subcontract, in which the con-
tracting agency is clearly in a superior or ruling
position. In such a case, the award of the bid in the
first place is considered to be a matter of benevolence—
an on. The nature of any discussion which might follow
fully reflects the existence of an oyabun-kobun
relationship:[2]

> In Japanese public construction contracts, just
> as in traditional tenant farming, it is normal
> for private construction businessmen to petition
> (chinjō), appeal to (tongan), and entreat

---

[1]Ibid., p. 14.   [2]Ibid., p. 11.

(kongan) the government when a problem arises,
and in return government agencies respond to
this attitude by not rejecting requests on the
ground of contractual legal relationships, then
more or less compromising with the businessmen
after such consultation.

In all cases of contract dispute, encouragement
is given to conciliation. In Japan, a situation exists
which is probably not markedly different from that in
many other countries: the existence of strong personal
ties, reinforced by social pressures to eschew
litigiousness, makes it possible for the terms of a
contract to go unmet without undue repercussion.
Japan is unique, however, in the fact that this informal
and personal element to the contract relationship has
been validated by the formal legal system. Court
opinions have, in effect, given legal sanction to the
customary aspect of "contract" in Japan whose authority
springs from amae.[1]

b. Right vs. Duty

The above characteristics point to the second
basis for the distinction between Japanese and western
understanding of contract: the difference between
right (e.g., to demand performance), and duty (e.g., to
conciliate).

_____

[1]For a detailed study of the operation of customary law in the conciliation of Tokugawa village contracts, see Dan Fenno Henderson, Village "Contracts" in
Tokugawa Japan (Seattle: University of Washington
Press, 1975).

In western society, the basic social unit is
the individual person; legally, "god-given rights"
inhere in and "state-given rights" adhere to the individual. In Japanese law also, rights are guaranteed to
the individual; societally, however, the basic social
unit has remained the group.

It is from the deprecatory attitude toward
"individualism" that litigiousness derives its dis-
tastefulness. Even today, a person who pursues a
matter into civil court is sometimes seen as one who
must either be overly concerned with his own (selfish)
interests, or so insensitive to human feelings as to
bring outsiders (i.e., the public courts) into what
must by its very existence be defined as a "family
affair."[1] To a Japanese, the controls of on-giri-ninjo
would appear to have been lost in such a situation.

Within that society whose interactions and
norms have been described in previous chapters, individual "rights" have far to go before approaching the
importance attached to duties and obligations among
interdependent people. Yet because of the reciprocal
nature of those duties in amae, they become in a real
sense "rights" among mutually dependent people.

---

[1] This same perception is largely responsible for
the failure of the concept of trial by jury of peers
to take hold in Japan.

Taking all these aspects of amae together, then, amae may be defined as the "right, duty and freedom" to be indulged by and to impose upon certain people.[1]

B. Individualism and Rights Consciousness

The reason for the continuing attachment to such traditional behavior patterns as on-giri is the strength of amae. Doi, however, finds the strength of those controls waning. If that is the case, we may expect to find evidence of increased individualism and increased assertion of individual "selfhood." The search for such evidence, among other things, has brought attention to the development of "rights consciousness" in Japan, and to the shimin undō whose activism bespeaks--at first glance, at least--its realization.

1. Selfhood

As has been stated, lack of "selfhood," a well-developed self-identity, is characteristic of personalities in the amae culture. The most outspoken members of Japanese society might well be looked to as the vanguard of a new selfhood. Ever since the opening of Japan to western writings, the student consciousness

---

[1]Conversation with Lawrence W. Beer, April 20, 1976.

has been the battlefront between new ideas and old.
Smith's characterization of the Taisho youth might
apply equally well to students of today (and in
countries other than Japan): "From a focus on the
'nation' emerges a stress on the 'self,' whether in the
form of the selfish acquisition of wealth (the "success
youth" or seiko seinen) or of existentialist despair
(the "anguishing youth" or hammon seinen)."

The expression used by students today to characterize their own activism is shutaisei, a term which
conveys meanings of both "selfhood" and "social
commitment."[2] The adoption of such a by-word, however,
is better understood not as a revolutionary attitude
but as part of the process of inter-generational value
changes discussed by Krauss.[3] A second quotation from
Smith's study of the Shinjinkai students of half a
century ago suggests that the content as well as the
occurrence of such value changes is constant: "It
would be fairer to portray this generation as 'self-
concerned' rather than 'selfish,' as seeking within the
individual a standard which the nation no longer
provided."[4]

---

[1]Smith, pp. x-xi.   [2]Krauss, p. 68.

[3]Ibid., pp. 12-15.   [4]Smith, p. xii.

From our examination of student radicalism it
was apparent that "selfhood" is not characteristic of
student activists psychologically. The group dynamics
and the susceptibility of students to the self-denial
involved in victim consciousness show that amae and its
attendant lack of selfhood in the western sense are
still widely shared.

2. Individualism

The new populism which some find in the growing
citizens' movements of the 1970's has been hailed as an
advance in "participatory democracy" in Japan.[1] That
perception probably includes the assumption that citizens joining together in loose, voluntary organizations
to represent their common interests are acting upon new
values of individualism and personal autonomy. That
assumption is not borne out.

a. Citizens' Movements

In the first place, groups presenting their
grievances to corporate or governmental officials is
not a new phenomenon. The presentation of petitions to
han magistrates occurred throughout the early Tokugawa
period. In one form, the "legal complaint" (shusō) was
presented by one village leader; but it represented the

---

[1]For a full discussion of the organizational
characteristics and tactics of contemporary shimin undō
in the framework of a critique of existing theories about
their revolutionary character, please see my "Citizens'
Movements in Contemporary Japan: The Politics of Localism," unpublished, University of Colorado, 1974.

plea of the entire community--most commonly seeking to lighten their tax burden. In the eyes of Tokugawa law, such a presumption on the part of a peasant was an affront punishable by beheading. In some cases, however, the petition was received with human feelingness, the request was considered in light of the extenuating circumstances (flood, drought) which may have related to the petition, and indulgence was shown in the handling of the request. In all cases, of course, the petition was presented with the utmost humility (and understandably, fear).

A second form, "mob appeal" (gōsō), grew to be favored in later Tokugawa. It had the advantage of making a complaint known to the official with jurisdiction, while at the same time bringing his unharmonious if not incompetent administration to the attention of his superiors. Accordingly, ameliorative action was more likely to be won. Usually, resort to mob appeal only followed the frustration of shusō or other less violent means of seeking relief.[1]

---

[1] In distinguishing the various forms of peasant uprisings (hyakushō ikki), Hugh Borton, Peasant Uprisings in Japan of the Tokugawa Period (New York: Paragon Book Reprint Corp., 1968) cites a detailed study by Aoki Koji. Chronological Study of Peasant Uprisings (1966), pp. 10ff.

This profile of amaeru is mirrored in the attitudes shown by many citizens' groups today, somewhat overstated by Vogel as follows:[1]

> Most Mamachi residents are uncertain about the rights of citizens vis a vis the government and think that it is rude or senseless to try to oppose an official on the basis of regulation. They believe that it is not might or law that makes right, but position.

Accordingly, contact with officials is generally avoided, but when political action is finally taken, "political groups present petitions and protests to their superiors or to society as a whole with an amae mentality, presuming on the good will and indulgence of the Japanese 'family'...and appealing for benevolent response."[2]

It is also indicative of the non-revolutionary character of these groups that "even large delegations do not expect to receive much consideration unless they are introduced by a person of power or position in that bureau."[3] If citizens' rights are being defended, it is being done not in the self-assertive manner borne of confidence in the democratic process so much as in the manner of amae, with confidence in being able to impose on particular individuals in the trust that their request will be considered with indulgence.

---

[1]Vogel (1963), p. 96.   [2]Beer (1976).

[3]Vogel (1963), p. 97.

In the second instance, the blockading and picket lines that have been identified with the shimin undō (for example, barring the entrance of workers into a polluting factory in Niihama Ehime, or blocking the entrance of garbage trucks into a landfill site in Setagaya district of Tokyo) are not usually the first tactics used. Such demonstrations follow periods of unresponsiveness to requests already made and are intended to call attention to the non-conciliatory and selfish position of the decision-makers (and perhaps, like their Tokugawa counterparts, to bring pressure to bear from superiors, as well as from the public). Some observers may confuse increased articulation of self-interest with a heightened self-awareness; in fact, the staging of demonstrations indicates that citizens concerned have been frustrated at an earlier point in their wish to amaeru.[1]

---

[1] It is interesting to note one tactic in particular of citizens' groups protesting pollution damage caused by a corporation. That is the "one share-holder movement" in which citizens purchase one share each of public stock in the corporation concerned in order to gain entrance to annual stockholders' meetings. Protestors' demands to be heard are ignored and become disruptive; companies hire professional thugs to police the meetings and to subdue trouble-makers. The greatest threat posed by dissident stockholders, however, is in the fact that because of their outspoken opposition to management policy, it is no longer possible for the affected company to report in minutes and annual reports that the agenda was approved unanimously. (Routinely, in fact, such business is rarely even brought to a vote.) The management is thus forced to display openly the fact of disunity among its "group." That this is the overriding source of concern is reflected in Keidanren's recent proposal of a minimum shareholding qualification to vote at such meetings, but not to restrict simple attendance. Japan Economic Journal, 13, No. 681, January 13, 1976), p. 4.

Among those citizens' groups combatting environmental pollution (kogai), the most effective have been the groups of people suffering from pollution-related disorders (caused, for example, by mercury poisoning). As victims (higaisha) in an entirely uncontrived sense, the members of one of these groups have been the beneficiaries of the largest damage award ever paid by a polluting company. The Chisso Corporation's actions in going beyond the payment of ¥930 million ordered by the Kumamoto District Court to 138 Minamata disease victims testifies to their sensitivity to victim status as characterized psychologically by Doi: not having been allowed to amaeru. Other groups, who do not yet bear the scars of pollution-related injury, but who nevertheless inhabit areas plagued with contaminated waters or fouled air, have capitalized on this "victim consciousness" and are presenting themselves not as "protest groups," but as "victim groups."

Third, despite considerable speculation, there is no reason to conclude at this point that voluntary organizations formed along the lines of shimin undō represent group formation patterns of newly autonomous individuals. Granted Nakane's claim that "in Japan it is very difficult to form and maintain the sort of

---

[1]Supra., p. 144, n. 1.

voluntary associations found so often in western
societies, in that it does not have the basis of frame
or existing vertical personal relations;"[1] nevertheless, her discussion throughout is in reference to
primary group formation. The group within the mainstream of shimin undō does not expect to have much
longevity, and it   certainly does not always corre-
spond to a primary group. Horizontal groups may
function successfully, according to Nakane, where they
are small, homogenous, and where each member knows
everyone else.[2] Certainly this would describe most
local and unaffiliated citizens' groups.[3] Therefore,
the phenomenon of shimin undō provides no evidence for
a significant movement toward individualism. And when
considered together with the above description of the
contract relationship, it seems that neither of the
alternative modes suggested by Nakane for group formation (horizontal or contractual) is viable.

In respect to rights consciousness, however, the
impact of shimin undō may be seen not so much in their

---

[1]Nakane, p. 59.   [2]Ibid., p. 62-63.

[3]Groups affiliated with larger, nationally or
regionally organized associations, such as the National
Federation of Regional Womens' Organizations (Chifuren),
seem to be organized along characteristic and formal
hierarchical lines; in fact, membership is loosely
defined and communications among such groups rely
primarily on the public media.

public demonstrations as in the increase in successful litigation brought against construction firms, public utilities, and government agencies.

b. Rights Litigation and Related Gains in Rights Consciousness

Environmental groups in particular have used to advantage the notion of "rights" in pressing their causes: from the "right to sunshine" to the "right to prevent undue disruption of environmental profits." Most claims of an "environmental right" may be seen as derivative of the guarantees contained in Article 25 of the Constitution:[1]

> All people shall have the right to maintain the minimum standards of wholesome and cultured living.
>
> In all spheres of life, the State shall use its endeavors for the promotion and extension of social welfare and security, and of public health.

Further evidence of growing "rights conscious-ness" is found in the increased resort to civil litiga-tion to block such environmental threats as the con-struction of a power plant, the building of a high-rise apartment, the routing of a highway through an

---

[1]The Constitution of Japan, Article 25.

area, as well as to enforce improved emission and noise control standards.[1]

Increasingly, courts are being persuaded by residents' claims to rightful input into decisions affecting their communities and livelihoods. In May 1973 the Kobe District Court made an important affirmation of a residents group's legal standing to seek a prior injunction against a highway construction company.[2]

Although the language of the courts seems to echo a heightened rights consciousness, the basis of decisions in favor of environmental groups does not appear to be concerned with individual rights per se, but the judgment that the views of citizens to be affected by a given enterprise--as a group-- warrant solicitation and attention. For example, the Urawa District Court in 1971 ordered a builder to pay ¥500,000 damages to three plaintiffs who claimed loss of sunshine from a four-story building. The court reasoned that the builder should have foreseen the trouble that would be caused for the neighbors, and

---

[1]For a comprehensive report on the status of pollution law in Japan, see Robert L. Seymour, "Environmental Law in Japan: Statutes and Cases," paper presented at the Western Conference, Association for Asian Studies, October, 1975.

[2]Japan Times, May 21, 1973; p. 2.

that he should have constructed the building differently
so as to avoid it.[1] Judgments of this sort show that
primary concern is for a "harmonizing" approach to be
taken in respect to potential environmental issues; the
sanctions of the court are directed primarily at those
parties who do not follow an appropriately conciliatory
path in either anticipating or meeting those issues.

So it has come about that legal rights of
citizen advocacy protected by the formal system have
developed from holdings which reflect fully the moral
rights of group-based consultation sustained by the
informal system of amae.

Significantly, the success of environmental
groups in obtaining satisfaction from the courts has
resulted in a recent mushrooming of damage claims in
unrelated areas, notably defamation and violation of
privacy cases.[2]

This tendency is an especially important
development in rights consciousness, since it seems to
be an assertion of individual rights in the face of
a "right" of much longer standing exercised by the

---

[1]Japan Times, June 25, 1971; p. 2.

[2]This is a trend noted by Beer on the basis of
the experience since 1971 of the Tokyo District Court.

group "to know about and to intrude freely in most any aspect of the life of the individual."[1]

3. Response to Activism: Restoration in the
   Symmetry of _Amae_

The response of government and business to the upsurge in popular activism has been made in such a way as to lessen as much as possible the impact of citizens' groups in drawing corporate affairs into the public realm, and to reinforce instead the more traditional willingness to trust leaders to act (privately) in consonance with the public welfare. As such, the doctrine of "social responsibility of corporations" is a modern day adaptation to the _amae_ relationship between the governed and the governing.

This type of response finds its expression in the Law on Special Measures for the Relief of Pollution-Related Injury (1969), enacted pursuant to the Basic Law for Poluttion Control.[2] Wishing to avoid the unsettling private law disputes in the difficult matter of ascertaining clear responsibility for pollution injury, the Special Measures provided for

---

[1]Lawrence W. Beer, "Defamation, Privacy, and Freedom of Expression in Japan," _Law_ _in_ _Japan_: _An_ _Annual_, vol. 5 (1972), p. 196.

[2]Kanazawa Yoshio, "A System of Relief for Pollution-Related Injury," _Law_ _in_ _Japan_: _An_ _Annual_, vol. 6 (1973), p. 65.

relief of such injury and costs of its treatment by
administrative determination of a Pollution Victims
Investigation Board. Payments to eligible victims were
to be made by local government, with costs largely
defrayed by a Pollution Control Association. This body
was to draw its funds from national tax revenues and
from a "private interest association" whose task it was
to collect from industries the funds needed to meet
their financial share of Pollution Control Association
awards. The public interest corporation had no power
to compel payment by industries. This arrangement
represented a compromise with industry by which its
"social responsibility" was upheld and in which no
liability was formally determined and no compulsion
existed to pay. Of course, since remedy was still
available through civil courts, such determination could
have been made through that process, resulting in still
greater costs to the company concerned. This consideration no doubt helped bring about the compromise with
those industries who first maintained that they should
be expected to bear none of the costs at all.[1]

This exercise in "social responsibility" has
been criticized as approaching too closely the use of
inadequate solatia called mimaikin, used to "mollify

---

[1]Ibid., passim.

victim grievances and restore harmony."[1] In that
respect, the 1969 law may be seen as a victory for
reticent companies in taking advantage of the exploitative potential of amae, since "the sole underpinning
for the /law/ is trust in the integrity of industry."[2]

Granted that the 1969 law was an important and
innovative response to critical area of need, the
replacement of that law with the 1973 Law for the Compensation of Pollution-related Health Damage represents
a stronger expression of industry's "social
responsibility." As a "mixed system" integrating administrative no-fault compensation and available judicial
remedy, the law provides for funding by mandatory
pollution levies which are imposed on the basis of a
liability principle which industry finds discomfitting.[3]
By laying responsibility for ecological destruction as
squarely as possible at the feet of those profitting
from it, while providing a face-saving administrative
buffer against direct liability, the government has
acted to chaige the concept of "social responsibility
of corporaticns" from a shibboleth to a reality.

---

[1]Julian Gresser, "The 1973 Japanese Law for the
Compensation of Pollution-related Health Damage: An
Introductory Assessment," Law in Japan: An Annual.
vol. 8 (1975). p. 98.

[2]Kanaziwa, p. 72.

[3]Gresser, pp. 109, 126.

Finally, it is interesting to note that the in-group protectiveness of industry seems almost xenophobic in recent <u>Keidanren</u> opposition to the stipulation of "social responsibility of corporations" in the Commercial Code presently under revision by the Ministry of Justice.[1]

The readjustment over time in the accountability of leaders in the private sector (with the term "private" used advisedly) to the public whose lives their decisions affect is a positive development which might well be emulated elsewhere. In Japan it does not represent a strengthening of "western" or individualistic values or a retreat from the dependency values of <u>amae</u>. Rather, it signifies the restoration of symmetry in the <u>amae</u> pattern which is perennially present. Public assertiveness does not necessarily represent new self-interest, but instead, increased demand for group consultation and observance of the rules of <u>amae</u>. Nevertheless, several important changes do seem to have occurred. First, the identity of the "group" whose <u>amae</u> freedoms are being increasingly exercised in contemporary Japan is being formulated more than before in terms of local, regional, and national citizenship.[2] Second, the increased assertion of the

---

[1]<u>Japan Economic Journal</u>, 13, No. 681. January 1976, p. 4.

[2]This conclusion is supported by Ishida. p.

rights of _amae_ is due in part to the increased awareness of the value of _amae_ in Japanese society, of its operation in human relations in all spheres--social, political, economic, and most importantly, of its reciprocal nature.

CHAPTER VII

CONCLUSION:

THE CONCEPT OF AMAE

The concept of "dependency," as a factor in
human behavior with important political impact is not
unique to Doi's analysis of the Japanese psychology.
Dependency in one sense is enjoying renewed attention
among political developmentalists studying "corporative"
governments.[1] The centralized state which embraces all
areas of social endeavor, however, is nourishing itself
on "dependency needs" of a totally different sort from
the expressive needs of the Japanese to amaeru.

Dependency is a term which may be encountered
frequently in the study of Japan, and especially in
the context of her history and her international relations. As one example, Maruyama finds dependency to
be at the heart of the Tokugawa adaptation of the following Confucian precept: "The people should be made
to depend upon /the Way/ but not be informed about it."[2]

---

[1]See for example H. J. Wiarda, "Toward a Framework for the Study of Political Change in the Iberic-
Latin Tradition: The Corporative Model," World Politics,
25 (1973), 206-235.

[2]Maruyama Masao, Studies in the Intellectual His-
tory of Tokugawa Japan (Tokyo: University of Tokyo
Press, 1974), p. 330, n. 4. From Analects, Book 8,
Chapter 9.

The use in this context of the verb yorashimu, meaning
to "depend passively," shows clearly that all
"dependency" in Japan is not amae. Japan is dependent
upon oil for the health of her economy; and with almost
ninety-nine percent of her oil needs imported, it may
very truthfully be said that Japan is dependent upon the
oil-producing nations. To say that Japan experiences an
amae relationship with those countries, however, would
not be correct. Nevertheless, Frank Gibney, who has
done more to distort the concept of amae than to clarify
it, draws such a conclusion after finding Japan to be
strategically, technologically, and commercially
"dependent" on the United States.[1]

The facility with which the language of dependency
is applied in political contexts makes it all the more
important to distinguish clearly the concept of amae by
describing as accurately as possible the operation of
amae in the social and political behavior of the Japanese.
In order to present the most concrete and comprehensive

---

[1]Gibney, p. 122. This is not to deny that
elements of the contract relationship between nations
do not introduce amae in foreign relations. The study
of amae in this context might meet Olson's call for
research into "foreign policy and decision-making from
a cultural-anthropological or socio-psychological point
of view." Lawrence Olson, Review of United States Japanese Relations in the 1970's, ed., Priscilla Clapp and
Morton Halperin, Journal of Asian Studies, 35, No. 1
(1975), 147.

picture of amae, in the absence of direct observation
or experience, I have drawn on the writings of scholars
from a variety of disciplines: psychiatry, psychology,
anthropology, sociology, law, and political science.
The integration of all these perspectives has led to a
more sophisticated understanding of amae in all its
complexities; and it has demonstrated the value of
multi-disciplinary approaches to cross-cultural
analysis.[1]

In the process of making the synthesis which this
study has presented, I have necessarily been selective.
The most important perspectives on amae which this
study has incorporated--and substantially supports--are
the cultural anthropological understanding of Befu,
the psycho-cultural interpretation of DeVos, and the
socio-psychological viewpoint of Beer. The latter may
be seen as an integration of Doi's and Nakane's
respective analyses. The perspectives of these and
many other writers all bring different points to light,
suggest different conclusions--some compatible and
others not, and raise different analytical considerations.

---

[1]For a discussion of disciplinary approaches and
their interrelationships in area studies, please see
Lucian W. Pye, ed., Political Science and Area Studies:
Rivals or Partners? (Bloomington: Indiana University
Press, 1975), especially selections by Pye and Robert
E. Ward, who address the problems particularly in the
field of East Asian studies.

In my efforts to draw my own conclusions from these
diverse strains, I have grappled with the following
problem perhaps more than any other: Is it more
helpful to understand amae as a cultural trait, a
social value, a personal motivational factor, or even
as an "indigenous value-institutional structure"?[1]
This is a question whose answer might be useful in
comparative theory-building; however, it is a question
to whose answer contemporary social science literature
seems to bring us woefully little closer.

A. The Unfolding of Amae: Concrete and Conceptual

In Chapter 2 I summarized the research of a
variety of scholars who have investigated the social
and child-rearing patterns which they found characteristic of Japanese families. In the process, each
had to address the conceptual problem of whether the
cultural or the parental influences were the greater
(over and above considerations of genetic inheritance).
Caudill and Weinstein determined that[2]

> out of the direct awareness of mother and child,
> the precursors of certain ways of behaving,
> thinking and feeling that are characteristic of
> a given culture have become part of an infant's

---

[1]Robert A. Scalapino, The Japanese Communist
Movement 1920-1966 (Berkeley: University of California
Press, 1967), p. 331.

[2]Caudill and Weinstein, 16.

207

approach to his environment well before the
development of language and hence are not
easily accessible to consciousness or to change.

Their conclusion points to the inseparability of the

two influences, but seems at the same time to attribute

much more importance to culture as its values are

transmitted non-verbally by parents than as it may

later act as an agent of changing values in a con-

sciously transmitted process. This is a position

which finds considerable opposition from socialization

theorists like Ellis Krauss,[1] whose de-emphasis of

family influence in a changing society is representative

of an approach to be mentioned briefly below.

Befu's understanding is that amae is primarily

parentally determined, and culturally determined only

insofar as the child-rearing practices of the parents

are culturally determined. His analysis is not an

equivocation, but a recognition of the interrelation

that must inevitably exist. He does not seem to allow,

however, for the fact that even children whose parents

may have brought them up in different ways from the

norm will be affected by that norm. For example, a

---

[1]Krauss (1974), on the basis of follow-up inter-
views among the Ampo student radicals of the early
1960's, discards the "red-diaper baby" theory as an
explanation for ideological extremism. His inquiry into
socialization in Japan is provocative, but leaves
unaddressed many fundamental questions about
consensually-held values.

child who does not receive the nurturance from his
mother that most of his friends do will nevertheless
learn the value of nurturance from his experience
outside the family. And because he learns from friends
that most mothers are viewed in a certain way, he also
views his mother according to that norm (with necessary
reinforcement from her occasional conformity with it).

Given that consensus exists on certain values,
a second question may be posed: are these
values in the realm of "culture" or "society"? Kroeber
and Parsons find society and culture to be "two distinct
systems in that they abstract or select two analytically
distinct sets of components from the same concrete
phenomena."[1] Thanks to that mode of analysis, despite
what preference one might have today for getting down
to those "concrete phenomena," the distinction remains
significant because of the difference in approach taken
by the sociologist and the cultural anthropologist,
among others.

In mapping the influence of amae, this study has
benefitted especially from the approach of the anthropologist, who, "influenced more or less directly by
Freud, sought the origins of stereotyped adult behavior

---

[1]A. L. Kroeger and Talcott Parsons, "The Concept
of Culture and of Social System," American Sociological
Review, 23, No. 5 (1958), 582.

in the emotional interactions between children and their

mothers, and other significant figures in their early

upbringing."[1]   Accordingly, I have made myself answerable

to the criticism of Barnlund:[2]

> Infants needs are not necessarily adult needs.
> Nor are habitual responses to those needs
> carried unaltered into adult life.... If infants
> have greater needs for security, for nurturance,
> for protection, for comfort, adults may be more
> strongly driven by needs for identity, for
> achievement, for social acceptance, or for
> prestige.
>
> Adults are more than simply large infants;
> the limited perceptions and limited means of
> expression of the child are replaced by wider
> perceptions and more subtle means of
> communicating.

His points are valid ones, and my agreement with them

is seen in Chapter 3. There (pp. 67-69), I showed the

continuities that exist in authority relationships

from the level of the family to that of the state. My

purpose, however, was not to find infantile drives

projected onto political symbols (although this may be

occurring), but rather to show that authority in the

political realm is maintained in the same way as in the

family. The unity of the family-state system was

supported by the belief in the value of the reciprocity

of amae.

---

[1]G. M. Carstairs, "Man's Social and Cultural
World," The Interface Between Psychiatry and Anthropology, ed. Iago Galdston (New York: Brunner/Mazel,
1970), p. 14.

[2]Barnlund, p. 110.

What I have done is to synthesize DeVos's insights into the reciprocal amae-sunao nature of authority relationships in Japan (pp. 74-75) with the "child-rearing approach" used in earlier studies in order to achieve a broader understanding of amae. Amae is significant to political behavior not simply because it is an emotional need carried over from childhood, and not simply because patterns of interaction acquired in the family are duplicated in the political sphere, but because amae is the unwritten basis for the legitimacy of authoritative rule in Japan.[1]

It is in the following sense that amae--in all its facets--is tremendously significant in the process of socialization to the political culture of Japan:[2]

> The most critical determinants of personality, and those most resistant to change, are found in patterns of infant care. Socialization occurs in the early weeks of life, and this means socialization to a specific cultural pattern.

---

[1]In terms of Barnlund's critique, consensus on the value of amae allows the "adult" needs--for example, for achievement--to be met in a manner which still gives expression to more basic, "infantile" needs. The fact that the discovery of this relationship was made by identifying amae as a key basic need and by linking its reciprocity to the experience of guilt should not be used prejudicially to dismiss an explanation which comports with experience.

Granted that DeVos may appear to argue at times that an achievement need would have no existence apart from amae, one need not accept this over-simplification in order to find merit in his over-all conclusions.

[2]Barnlund, p. 97.

To me, that concrete expression of the experience which
each child undergoes within the family and without shows
the limited value of the distinction between the "social"
system and the culture to which one is "social"-ized.[1]

---

[1]Apparently in an attempt to perpetuate this
analytical distinction, socialization theorists have
built an increasingly narrow conceptualization of
"political socialization." The barrenness of leading
research in socialization theory is revealed by asser-
tions that parents are not the primary agents of political socialization. /Kent L. Tedin, "The Influence of
Parents on the Political Attitudes of Adolescents,"
American Political Science Review, 68, No. 4 (1974),
1579./ Primary defenders of this hypothesis have been
Hess and Torney /Robert Hess and Judith Torney, The
Development of Political Attitudes in Children (Chicago:
Anchor Press, 1967)/, who selected as their objects of
study the attitudes of children in their relationships
to the nation, authority figures, legal institutions,
enforcement figures, decision-making processes, parties
and elections (p. 212). After evaluating family
influence on attitudes held within those several "relationships," the authors concluded that "Aside from party
preference, the influence of the family seems to be
primarily indirect and to influence attitudes toward
authority, rules and compliance" (p. 217). This failure
to clarify or address the full significance of "indirect"
influence on such fundamental values as obedience seems
to stem from an overly narrow and behavioristically
defined concept of political culture. Such an approach
in Japan would ignore the political significance of the
fundamental value of amae, which is a basis for
legitimacy within that political system. Richard
Merelman /"Learning and Legitimacy," American Political
Science Review, 60, No. 3(1966), 552/ seemed to take
socialization theory in a direction toward a renewed
appreciation of such factors when he attested that
"legitimacy, or its opposites, is one of the first
political attitudes evident in children."
     More critically, the concept of political sociali-
zation itself, being kept distinct from socialization
per se, is unnecessarily and artificially restricted.
If, as I have argued, a sense of what is and what is not
legitimate rule is one of the most important--and
enduring--political values acquired in the family, then
there seems to be small gain in testing, as Krauss and
others have done, parental impact on changes in party
preference or voting behavior, without giving due recognition to the political impact of earlier socializing
experiences in the family as described above by Barnlund.

The rigor of behaviorists has been corrective at least. By acknowledging the roots of DeVos's theory in the dynamics of personal guilt, I may be open, next, to Durkheim's criticism: "Whenever a social phenomenon is directly explained by a psychological phenomenon, we may be sure that the explanation is false."[1] However, the psychological cause-and-effect patterns outlined by Doi and his adherents are hardly the simplistic mechanisms which, seventy-five years ago, were worthy of the sociologist's skepticism. In the second place, I decline to be intimidated by those who adhere even today to a misdirected purism. As has been pointed out elsewhere,[2] even those (pre-eminently, Levi-Strauss) who purport to explain social customs only in terms of social structure and functions nevertheless "presuppose hidden structures, principles, or symbolic elements"[3] which must be congruent with the human psyche in order to be operative in human

---

[1]E. D. Wittkower and Guy Dubreuil, "Reflections on the Interface Between Psychiatry and Anthropology." The Interface Between Psychology and Anthropology, ed. Iago Galdston (1970), pp. 5-6.

[2]For a refreshingly irreverent critique of grand theorizing and methodological obfuscation, see Stanislav Andreski, Social Sciences as Sorcery (New York: St. Martin's Press, 1972). Primary among the grand sorcerers (second, perhaps, only to Parsons) is Levi-Strauss, who is taken to task on pages 83-85 and passim.

[3]Wittkower and Dubreuil, 6.

groups. Since they are hidden from the actors themselves, they must be based on unconscious psychological
mechanisms which can be found only in each individual.

In Chapter 4, the operation of reciprocal amae
was described in the intermediate social groups
between family and nation. The structural patterns of
group formation (pp. 83-84) and the organizational
imperatives of consensus-building (pp. 96-98) were
shown to insure full emotional commitment to the
in-group by facilitating the expression and gratification of amae needs. In arguing for the "explanatory
power" of amae, however, I have been mindful of
Silberman's suggestion that[1]

> patterns of organizational behavior in Japan
> often thought to be reflections of the persistance
> of traditional norms and values deserve closer
> scrutiny in terms of organizational theory and
> comparative analysis. It may well be that such
> patterns can be more readily and efficiently
> explained in terms of universal organizational
> responses to historical problem situations than
> in terms of generalized functionalist theory.

By bringing together the structural theory of
Nakane and the psychiatrical theory of Doi, I have gone
beyond a "functional" description of groups such as
political factions in Japan. While granting that historical conditions at the end of World War II lent
themselves to factional divisions, I have attested to
the functional successes of a factionalized ruling

---

[1]Bernard Silberman, "Ringi-sei," 251.

party (pp. 111-113). I have also suggested that among the functions of factions, or of any in-group, is that of providing the means for the open expression of amae (pp. 120-122). But amae is significant to group behavior in additional ways. According to Nakane, the group is formed in keeping with what might very well be   recognized soon as a "universal organizational response" (after Silberman) to the emotional drives which Japanese--and perhaps untold others--bring into their work. Most importantly, however, the unspoken consensus on the value of reciprocal amae legitimizes the socio-political pressures on the individual to behave in conformity with the group demands of harmony and loyalty.

In Chapter 5 and 6 I selected two additional realms of political behavior--political opposition and the conciliation of legal rights--in order to show the full extent of the consensus which exists on the value of amae and the degree to which it has been incorporated as a basis for legitimacy not only within the "informal"

social hierarchy of Japan, but within the "formal"
political-legal structure as well.[1]

B. Conclusion

In conclusion, amae is many things. It is a
strong emotional dependency built in the mother-child
relationship. Learned as a "preferred moral behavior"
which is the basis of customary law, it has been
internalized as a personal motivational factor.[2] Or as
a shared emotional urge, it has become a fundamental
cultural value that dictates the forms which interpersonal relations have taken.[3] Or still again it is
a dependency orientation built upon the antecedent
hierarchical nature of Japanese human relations.[4] The
argument which I have presented here reaches the following conclusion: Amae dependency is the primary
emotional content of interpersonal relations in Japan:

---

[1]For a theoretical discussion of legitimacy in
its relationship to both customary and judicial law,
see Leopold Pospisil, The Ethnology of Law, Modular
Publication No. 12 (Reading, Massachusetts: Addison-
Wesley Publishing Co., Inc., 1972). By the terms of his
analysis, Japan may be seen as especially unique among
modern nations for its unified "legal level," which
results from the congruency of moral, legal, and
political codes.

[2]Conversation with Lawrence W. Beer, January
1976.

[3]Doi (1973), p. 82.   [4]Befu (1975). 151.

its fullest possible expression, in society and politics,
and in both private and public relations, is valued as
the legitimate end of authoritative groups in Japan.

This conclusion represents a happy congruence
with the particularistic world-view of most Japanese,
who would very likely find puzzling, if not futile, my
effort to make generalizations about a necessarily
"limited human" experience. Bakke, in another context,
has given admirable expression to this concrete and
intersubjective experience of amae:[1]

> Its moral ingredients, so familiar and buttressed
> by customary behavior that they scarcely need to
> be vocalized, are the foundations for daily
> living subconsciously sensed as truly Japanese
> values.

Finally, I have argued that what distinguishes
the Japanese experience from others is not the need to
be dependent, but the degree to which the open expression of that need has been culturally encouraged and
politically institutionalized. In this respect, my
conclusion shows the extent to which freedom of
expression--in the manner of amae--exists as the
fundamental value of Japanese democracy today. The
fact that such a value has become institutionalized in
a society whose path to democracy has been largely
outside the liberal tradition testifies to the

---

[1]E. Wight Bakke, Revolutionary Democracy (Hamden,
Connecticut: Archon Books, 1968), p. 275.

existence of a universal human need for self-expression.[1]
My hope is that this study of _amae_ brings that pro-
foundly human need one step closer to accessibility
for comparative study and theoretical understanding.

---

[1]An argument for the existence of such a need
has been made persuasively by Christian Bay, The Structure of Freedom (New York: Atheneum, 1965); the
possibilities for its knowability have been argued for
by Abraham Maslow, The Farther Reaches of Human Nature
(New York: Viking Press, 1971).

LIST OF WORKS CONSULTED

Abegglen, James C. "Japanese Management After the Storm." The President Directory 1976. Tokyo: Diamond-Time Co., Ltd., 1975, pp. 10-17.

_____. Management and Worker: The Japanese Solution. Tokyo: Sophia University Press, 1973.

Austin, Lewis. Saints and Samurai: The Political Cultures of the American and Japanese Elites. New Haven: Yale University Press, 1975.

Babcock, Charlotte G. "Reflections on Dependency Phenomena as Seen in Nisei in the U.S." Japanese Culture. Eds. Robert J. Smith and Richard K. Beardsley. Chicago: Aldine Publishing Co., 1962.

Baerwald, Hans H. "An Aspect of Japanese Parliamentary Politics." Japan Interpreter, 6, No. 2 (1970), 196-205.

_____. Japan's Parliament: An Introduction. London: Cambridge University Press, 1974.

_____. "The Tanabata House of Councillors Election in Japan." Asian Survey, 14, No. 10 (1974), 900-906.

Bakke, E. Wight. Revolutionary Democracy. Hamden, Connecticut: Archon Books, 1968.

Barnlund, Dean C. Public and Private Self in Japan and the United States. Tokyo: The Simul Press, 1975.

Bay, Christian. The Structure of Freedom. 2d Edition. New York: Atheneum, 1965.

Bayley, David H. "The Future of Social Control in Japan." Unpublished, University of Denver, 1976.

Beardsley, Richard K. "Cultural Anthropology: Prehistoric and Contemporary Aspects." Twelve Doors to Japan. Ed. John W. Hall and Richard K. Beardsley. New York: McGraw-Hill, 1965; pp. 48-120.

_____. "Personality Psychology." Twelve Doors to Japan. Ed. John W. Hall and Richard K. Beardsley. New York: McGraw-Hill, 1965; pp. 350-83.

Beer, Lawrence W. "Defamation, Privacy, and Freedom of
Expression in Japan." Law in Japan, 5 (1972),
192-208.

_____. "Freedom of Expression in Japan with Com-
parative Reference to the United States." Comparative Human Rights. Ed. Richard P. Claude.
Baltimore: Johns Hopkins University Press, 1975.

_____. "Freedom of Information and the Evidentiary
Use of Film in Japan." American Political Science
Review, 65, No. 4 (1971), 1119-1132.

_____. "Japan 1969: 'My Homeism' and Political
Struggle." Asian Survey, 10, No. 1 (1970),
43-55.

_____. "Japan Turning the Corner." Asian Survey,
11, No. 1 (1971), 74-85.

_____. "The Public Welfare Standard and Freedom of
Expression in Japan." The Constitution of Japan:
Its First Twenty Years, 1947-1967. Ed. Dan
Fenno Henderson. Seattle: University of Wash-
ington Press, 1968; pp. 205-238.

Befu, Harumi. Japan: An Anthropological Introduction.
San Francisco: Chandler Publishing Co., 1971.

_____. Review of For Harmony and Strength, Thomas
P. Rohlen. Journal of Asian Studies, 35, No. 1
(1975), 150-152.

Benedict, Ruth. The Crysanthemum and the Sword. Boston:
Houghton-Mifflin, 1946.

Benjamin, Roger W. and Kan Ori. "Factionalism in Japanese Politics." Japan Institute of International
Affairs. Annual Review, 5 (1969/70), 76-91.

Bennett, John W. and Iwao Ishino. Paternalism in the
Japanese Economy: Anthropological Studies of
Oyabun-Kobun Patterns. Minneapolis: University
of Minnesota Press, 1963.

Bowen, Roger Wilson. "The Narita Conflict." Asian Survey, 15, No. 7 (1975), 598-615.

Brameld, Theodore. Japan; Culture, Education, and
Change in Two Communities. New York: Holt,
Rinehart and Winston, 1968.

Carstairs, G. M. "Man's Social and Cultural World."
The Interface between Psychology and Anthropology.
Ed. Iago Galdston. New York: Brunner/Mezel, 1970;
pp. 140-150.

Caudill, William. "Around the Clock Patient Care in
Japanese Psychiatric Hospitals: The Role of the
Tsukisoi." American Sociological Review, 26
(1961), 204-214.

_____. "Patterns of Emotion in Modern Japan." Jap-
anese Culture. Ed. Robert J. Smith and Richard
K. Beardsley. Chicago: Aldine Publishing Co.,
1962; pp. 115-131.

_____ and George Devos. "Achievement, Culture, and
Personality: The Case of the Japanese-Americans."
American Anthropologist, 58, No. 6 (1956), 1102-
1126.

_____ and Doi Takeo. "Interrelation of Psychiatry,
Culture, and Emotion in Japan." Man's Image in
Medicine and Anthropology. Ed. Iago Galdston.
New York: International University Press, 1963;
pp. 374-421.

_____ and David Plath. "Who Sleeps by Whom? Parent
-Child Involvement in Urban Japanese Families."
Psychiatry, 29 (1966), 344-366.

_____ .and Harry A. Scarr. "Japanese Value Orientation and Cultural Change." Ethnology, 1 (1962).
53-91.

_____ and Helen Weinstein. "Maternal Care and Infant Behavior in Japan and America." Psychiatry,
32 (1969), 12-43.

Clapp, Priscilla and Morton A. Halperin, eds. United
States-Japanese Relations in the 1970's. Cambridge: Harvard University Press, 1974.

Cole, Allan B., George O. Totten, and Cecil H. Uyehara.
Socialist Parties in Postwar Japan. New Haven:
Yale University Press, 1966.

Craig, Albert M. "Functional and Dysfunctional Aspects
of Government Bureaucracy." Modern Japanese
Organization and Decision-Making. Ed. Ezra F.
Vogel. Berkeley: University of California
Press, 1975; pp. 3-32.

Curtis, Gerald L. Election Campaigning Japanese Style.
New York: Columbia University Press, 1971.

Devos, George A. "Apprenticeship and Paternalism."
Modern Japanese Organization and Decision-Making.
Ed. Ezra F. Vogel. Berkeley: University of Cali-
fornia Press, 1975; pp. 210-227.

_____. Socialization for Achievement. Berkeley:
University of California Press, 1973.

Doi Takeo. "Amae: A Key Concept for Understanding Jap-
anese Personality Structure." Japanese Culture.
Eds. Robert J. Smith and Richard K. Beardsley.
Chicago: Aldine Publishing Co., 1962; pp. 132-139.

_____. The Anatomy of Dependence. Trans. John
Bester. Tokyo: Kodansha Int'l., Ltd., 1973.

_____. "Giri-Ninjo: An Interpretation." Aspects
of Social Change in Modern Japan. Ed. Ronald P.
Dore. Princeton: Princeton University Press,
1967; pp. 327-334.

_____. "Some Aspects of Japanese Psychiatry."
American Journal of Psychiatry, 3 (1955), 691-695.

Earhardt, H. Byron. Japanese Religion: Unity and Diversity. Encino, California: Dickenson Publishing
Co., Inc., 1974.

Freud, Sigmund. Civilization and Its Discontents. Ed.
James Strachey. New York: W. W. Norton and Co.,
Inc., 1961.

Fukui Haruhiro. Party in Power. Berkeley: University
of California Press, 1970.

Fukutake Tadashi. Japanese Rural Society. Trans. R. P.
Dore. London: Cornell University Press, 1972.

Gibney, Frank. Japan: The Fragile Superpower. New
York: W. W. Norton and Co., Inc., 1975.

Gluckman, Max. Politics, Law, and Ritual in Tribal
Society. Oxford: Basil Blackwell, 1965.

Gregory, Gene. "Japanese Economic Growth: The Human
Equation." Asian Survey, 15, No. 10 (1975),
851-869.

Gresser, Julian. "The 1973 Japanese Law for the Compen-
sation of Pollution-related Health Damage: An
Introductory Assessment." Law in Japan: An
Annual, 8 (1975), 91-135.

Hahm Pyong Choon. "The Decision Process in Korea."
Comparative Judicial Behavior: Cross-cultural
Studies of Political Decision-making in the East
and West. Eds. Glendon Schubert and David J.
Danelski. New York: Oxford University Press,
1969.

Hall, Robert King. Shūshin: The Ethics of a Defeated
Nation. New York: Columbia University Press,
1949.

Halloran, Richard. "The Fear is That Hard Times in
Japan Will be Permanent." New York Times, February 8, 1976, vi, p. 5.

_____. Japan: Images and Realities. New York:
Alfred A. Knopf, 1969.

Hane, Mikiso. Japan: A Historical Survey. New York:
Charles Scribner's Sons, 1972.

Henderson, Dan Fenno. Conciliation and Japanese Law:
Tokugawa and Modern. 2 vols. Seattle: University of Washington Press, 1965.

Hess, Robert and Judith Torney. The Development of Political Attitudes in Children. New York: Alfred
A. Knopf, 1969.

Ishida Takeshi. Japanese Society. New York: Random
House, 1971.

Ito Masami. "The Rule of Law: Constitutional Development." Law in Japan: The Legal Order in a
Changing Society. Ed. Arthur T. von Mehren.
Cambridge: Harvard University Press, 1963;
pp. 205-238.

Itoh, Hiroshi, ed. Japanese Politics - An Inside View.
Ithaca: Cornell University Press, 1973; pp. 3-
11.

Johnson, Chalmers. "Japan: Who Governs? An Essay on
Official Bureaucracy." Journal of Japanese
Studies, 2, No. 1 (1975), 1-28.

Jugaku Akiko. Characteristics of Japanese People Seen in the Peculiarities of Japanese Language. Japan Research Series, No. 5. Tokyo: Association of International Education, 1970.

Kahn, Herman. The Emerging Japanese Superstate. Englewood Cliffs, New Jersey: Prentice-Hall, Inc., 1970.

Kanazawa Yoshio. "A System of Relief for Pollution-Related Injury." Law in Japan: An Annual, 6 (1973), 65-72.

Kawashima Takeyoshi. "Dispute Resolution in Contemporary Japan." Law in Japan. Ed. Arthur T. von Mehren. Cambridge: Harvard University Press, 1963; pp. 41-72.

_____. "The Legal Consciousness of Contract in Japan." Law in Japan: An Annual, 7 (1974), 1-21.

King, Anthony. "Political Parties: Some Skeptical Reflections." Comparative Politics: Notes and Readings. Eds. Roy Macridis and Bernard Brown. Homewood, Illinois: Dorsey Press, 1972; pp. 233-251.

Kitano, Harry. Japanese Americans: The Evolution of a Subculture. Englewood Cliffs: Prentice-Hall, Inc., 1969.

Kluckhohn, Florence and Fred L. Strodtbeck. Variations in Value Orientations. Westport, Connecticut: Greenwood Press, 1961.

Kodama Yoshio. I Was Defeated. Tokyo: Radiopress, 1959.

Krauss, Ellis S. Japanese Radicals Revisited. Berkeley: University of California Press, 1974.

Kroeber, A. L. and Talcott Parsons. "The Concepts of Culture and of Social System." American Sociological Review, 23, No. 5 (1958), 582-3.

Kubota Akira. Higher Civil Servants in Postwar Japan. Princeton: Princeton University Press, 1969.

Kuroda, Alice and Yasumasa. "Aspects of Community Political Participation in Japan." Journal of Asian Studies, 27 (1968), 229-251.

Kuroda, Yasumasa. "Agencies of Political Socialization and Political Change." Human Organization, 24, No. 4 (1965-66), 328-31.

Lanham, Betty B. "Aspects of Child Care in Japan: A Preliminary Report." Personal Character and Cultural Milieu. Ed. Douglas G. Haring. Syracuse: Syracuse University Press, 1956; pp. 565-583.

Lasch, Christopher. "The Emotions of Family Life." New York Review, November 23, 1975; pp. 37-42.

Lifton, Robert J. Death in Life. New York: Random House, 1967.

Maslow, Abraham H. The Farther Reaches of Human Nature. New York: Viking Press, 1971.

Maruyama Masao. Studies in the Intellectual History of Tokugawa Japan. Tokyo: University of Tokyo Press, 1974.

_____. Thought and Behavior in Modern Japanese Politics. Ed. Ivan Morris. London: Oxford University Press, 1963.

May, Rollo. Love and Will. New York: W. W. Norton and Co., Inc., 1969.

McNelly, Theodore, ed. Sources in Modern East Asian History and Politics. New York: Appleton-Century-Crofts, 1967.

Mehren, Arthur T. von, ed. Law in Japan: The Legal Order in a Changing Society. Cambridge: Harvard University Press, 1963.

Merelman, Richard M. "Learning and Legitimacy." American Political Science Review, 60, No. 3 (1966), 548-561.

Misawa Shigeo. "An Outline of the Policy-Making Process in Japan." Japanese Politics - An Inside View. Ed. Hiroshi Itoh. Ithaca: Cornell University Press, 1973; pp. 12-48.

Mitchell, Douglas D. "Citizens Movements in Contemporary Japan: The Politics of Localism." Unpublished, University of Colorado, 1974.

_____. "The Value of Freedom of Expression in South Korea." Unpublished, University of Colorado, 1975.

Olson, Lawrence. Review of United States-Japanese Relations in the 1970's, ed. Priscilla Clapp and Morton H. Halperin. Journal of Asian Studies, 35, No. 1 (1975), pp. 145-47.

Nakane Chie. Japanese Society. Berkeley: University of California Press, 1970.

Nakamura Hajime. Ways of Thinking of Eastern Peoples. Ed. Philip P. Wiener. Honolulu: University of Hawaii Press, 1964.

Nitobe Inazo. Bushido. Tokyo: Teibi Publishing Co., 1908.

Norbeck, Edward and Margaret. "Child Training in a Japanese Fishing Community." Personal Character and Cultural Milieu. Ed. Douglas G. Haring. Syracuse: Syracuse University Press, 1956; pp. 651-673.

Packard, George R., III. Protest in Tokyo: The Security Treaty Crisis of 1960. Princeton: Princeton University Press, 1966.

Passin, Herbert. "Changing Values: Work and Growth in Japan." Asian Survey, 15, No. 10 (1975). 821-850.

Pospisil, Leopold. The Ethnology of Law. Modular Publication Series. Reading, Massachusetts: Addison-Wesley Publishing Co., Inc., 1972.

Pye, Lucian W., ed. Political Science and Area Studies. Rivals or Partners? Bloomington: Indiana University Press, 1975.

Rohlen, Thomas P. "The Company Work Group." Modern Japanese Organization and Decision-Making. Ed. Ezra F. Vogel. Berkeley: University of California Press, 1975; pp. 185-209.

_____. For Harmony and Strength: Japanese White-Collar Organization in Anthropological Perspective. Berkeley: University of California Press. 1974.

Sansom, George B. A History of Japan to 1334. Stanford Stanford University Press, 1958.

_____. A History of Japan, 1615 to 1867. Stanford Stanford University Press, 1963.

Scalapino, Robert A. Democracy and the Party Movement in Prewar Japan. Berkeley: University of California Press, 1953.

_____. The Japanese Communist Movement, 1920-1966. Berkeley: University of California Press, 1967.

_____ and Junnosuke Masumi. Parties and Politics in Contemporary Japan. Berkeley: University of California Press, 1962.

Schmitz, Tim J. "Japanese Intellectuals: Reactions to Modernization." Unpublished, University of Colorado, 1972.

Seymour, Robert L. "Environmental Law in Japan: Statutes and Cases." Unpublished, University of Colorado, 1975.

Silberman, Bernard S. "Bureaucratic Development and the Structure of Decision-Making in the Meiji Period." Journal of Asian Studies, 27, No. 1 (1967), 81-94.

_____. Ringi-sei: Traditional Values or Organizational Imperatives in the Japanese Upper Civil Service: 1868-1945." Journal of Asian Studies, 32, No. 2 (1973), 251-264.

Smith, Henry DeWitt, II. Japan's First Student Radicals. Cambridge: Harvard University Press, 1972.

Smith, Thomas C. The Agrarian Origins of Modern Japan. Stanford: Stanford University Press, 1959.

Solomon, Richard H. Mao's Revolution and the Chinese Political Culture. Berkeley: University of California Press, 1971.

Soseki Natsume. Light and Darkness. Trans. V. H. Viglielmo. Exeter: Peter Owen, Ltd., 1971.

Spaulding, Robert M., Jr. Imperial Japan's Civil Service Examinations. Princeton: Princeton University Press, 1967.

Starr, John Bryan. Ideology and Culture. New York: Harper and Row, 1975.

Stockwin, J.A.A. Japan: Divided Politics in a Growth Economy. New York: W. W. Norton and Co., Inc., 1975.

Stockwin, J.A.A. The Japanese Socialist Party and Neutralism. Carlton, Victoria: Melbourne University
Press, 1968.

Sunada Ichiro. "The Thought and Behavior of Zengakuren: Trends in the Japanese Student Movement."
Asian Survey, 9, No. 6 (1969), 457-474.

Suzuki Tatsuzo. "A Study of the Japanese National
Character, Part IV." Nipponzin No Kokuminsei
(II). Hayashi Chikio, Aoyama Hirojiro, Nisihira
Sigeki, and Suzuki Tatsuzo. Tokyo: The Insti-
tute of Statistical Mathematics, 1970.

"Symposium on Strong Points and Weaknesses of Japanese
Economy." Japan Economic Journal, December 30,
1975; p. 10.

Tedin, Kent L. "The Influence of Parents on the Political Attributes of Adolescents." American Political Science Review, 68, No. 4 (1974), 1579-1592.

Thayer, Nathaniel B. How the Conservatives Rule Japan.
Princeton: Princeton University Press, 1969.

Titus, David A. "Emperor and Public Consciousness in
Postwar Japan." Japan Interpreter, 6, No. 2
(1970), 182-195.

_____. Palace and Politics in Prewar Japan. New
York: Columbia University Press, 1974.

Totten, George O. and Kawakami Tamio. "The Functions of
Factionalism in Japanese Politics." Pacific
Affairs, 38, No. 2 (1965), 109-122.

Tsuji Kiyoaki. "Decision-Making in the Japanese Government: A Study of Ringisei." Political Development in Modern Japan. Ed. Robert E. Ward.
Princeton: Princeton University Press, 1968.

Tsurumi Kazuko. Social Change and the Individual:
Japan Before and After Defeat in World War II.
Princeton: Princeton University Press, 1970.

Vogel, Ezra F. Japan's New Middle Class. Berkeley:
University of California Press, 1963.

_____, ed. Modern Japanese Organization and Deci-
sion-making. Berkeley: University of California
Press, 1975; pp. xiii-xxv.

Weinstein, Fred and Gerald M. Platt. The Wish to be Free: Society, Psyche and Value Change. Berkeley: University of California Press, 1975.

Weisbrod, R.J.R. "Voluntary Organizations: A General Analysis Applied to the Japanese New Religions." Cornell Journal of Social Relations, 1, No. 2 (1966), 64-84.

White, James W. Review of Prologue to the Future: The United States and Japan in the Post-Industrial Age, ed. James W. Morley. Journal of Asian Studies, 35, No. 1 (1975), 147-48.

_____. "State Building and Modernization: The Meiji Restoration." Crisis, Choice, and Change: Historical Studies of Political Development. Eds. Gabriel A. Almond, Scott C. Flanagan, Robert J. Mundt. Boston: Little, Brown and Company, 1973; pp. 499-558.

Wittkower, E. D. and Guy Dubreuil. "Reflections on the Interface between Psychiatry and Anthropology." The Interface between Psychiatry and Anthropology. Ed. Iago Galdston. New York: Brunner/Mazel, 1970; pp. 1-27.

Yamanouchi Kazuo. "Administrative Guidance and the Rule of Law." Law in Japan: An Annual, 7 (1974), 22-33.